The
SPIRITUAL
QUEST

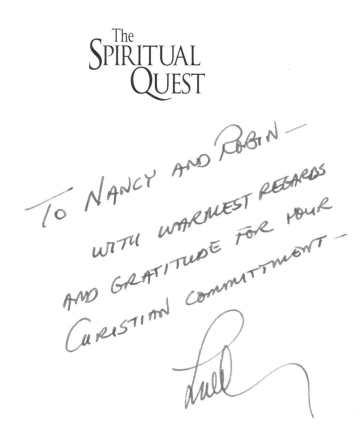

To Nancy and Robin —
with warmest regards
and gratitude for your
Christian commitment —

The SPIRITUAL QUEST

Pursuing
Christian
Maturity

Luder G. Whitlock Jr.

Baker Books
A Division of Baker Book House Co
Grand Rapids, Michigan 49516

© 2000 by Luder G. Whitlock Jr.

Published 1998 by Baker Books
a division of Baker Book House Company
P.O. Box 6287, Grand Rapids, MI 49516-6287

Second printing, December 2001

Printed in the United States of America

Library of Congress Cataloging-in-Publication Data

Whitlock, Luder G.
    The spiritual quest : pursuing Christian maturity / Luder G. Whitlock, Jr.
       p. cm.
    Includes bibliographical references (p.).
    ISBN 0-8010-6338-8 (paper)
    1. Christian life—Reformed authors. 2. Spiritual life—Reformed Church. 3. God—Attributes. I. Title.
    BV4501.2.W474 2000
    248.8'4—dc21   00-041468

For current information about all releases from Baker Book House, visit our web site:
                http://www.bakerbooks.com

To
my loving and faithful wife,
Mary Lou,
and to our three children
Chris, Alissa, and Beth

Contents

PREFACE

The Spiritual Quest is about encountering God, but it is about more than that. Spiritual seekers have a great deal of information available to them regarding the gospel that can guide them into an authentic relationship with God. Many books offer suggestions on how to grow spiritually. Devotional literature abounds.

With all of this information readily available and the increased interest in spirituality as of late, why don't we see a greater behavioral difference between church members and non-church members? It surely cannot be attributed to a high level of public virtue. If anything, morality seems to be in decline.

One major problem may be that Christians do not have a clear idea about how they should change. Many Christians seem unsure of the transformation God expects. If that is the case, any correlation between what they become and what God expects is purely coincidental.

Do you recall the following scene from *Alice in Wonderland*? Alice is in a quandary. She faces a fork in the road and does not know which path is the right one to take, so she asks the cat and he responds, "Where do you want to go?" Alice tells him she doesn't know. The cat replies, "Then either road will do."

If we expect Christians to attain spiritual maturity, then we must clearly describe what spiritual maturity looks like so that they know what they are striving for. This book is

9

a step in that direction, with the hope that it may become a valuable guide and encouragement to those who love the Lord and seek to glorify him.

I wish to acknowledge the contribution of those who helped make this volume possible. First, I am grateful to Robert Hosack, who persevered through many years, steadily encouraging me to commit these ideas to print. The Board of Trustees of Reformed Theological Seminary granted me a two-month leave so I could concentrate on this project. My wife, Mary Lou, has been a marvelous example of faith through the years and was extremely helpful with the writing and revision of this manuscript. My assistant, Alice Hopkins, was cheerfully tireless in working through details of manuscript revision.

I am also grateful to several friends and colleagues who read the manuscript and made helpful suggestions: Roger Nicole, Steve Brown, Rebecca Hobbs, John Muether, Howard and Trisha Edington, and Susan Nowlin.

I still see sections that cry for improvement, but life is like that too. We press and improve, correct and revise— only to discover many additional flaws and sins that clamor for remedy. Until we stand spotless before the Lamb in glory, it shall remain that way. Until then, let us continue in our quest for spiritual maturity.

CHAPTER ONE

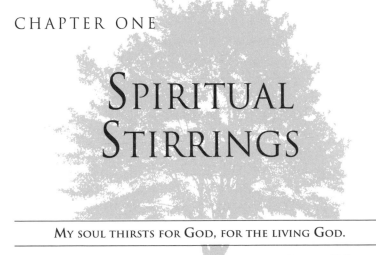

SPIRITUAL STIRRINGS

MY SOUL THIRSTS FOR GOD, FOR THE LIVING GOD.

PSALM 42:2

St. Augustine said it best: "You have made us for your-self, and our heart is restless until it rests in you."[1] As if in response to his observation, millions of Americans have embarked on a fresh search for the sacred, seemingly determined to continue until their inmost longings have been satisfied. Evidencing a hunger for God, their spiritual quest finds its center in a consuming interest in the inner life. During a recent conversation, George Gallup Jr. expressed his amazement at these spiritual stirrings in our country, observing that compared to prior years of research, there is currently an unparalleled level of interest in things spiritual.[2] These seekers are trying to connect

11

spiritually. They want to experience God personally. Modern-day pilgrims, they are marked by a common desire to discover answers to the profound questions of life:

Who am I?
How did I get here?
Where am I going?
What is my purpose in life?

The signs are unmistakably clear—something is happening. There is a resurgence of spiritual hunger. This should come as no surprise, for every person has an inner sense of deity or awareness of God that creates in him or her a religious drive. This inner longing for God may be triggered by a crisis such as death, divorce, loss of a job, or perhaps a midlife crisis that shatters what has been facilely assumed. Raw pain, numbing purposelessness, or nagging questions can awaken the slumbering soul. Whatever the reason, that spiritual drive is manifesting itself powerfully in the current religious stirrings that are sweeping this land.

Local bookstores are a good indicator of the high interest level in things spiritual, as volumes by Thomas Moore, James Redfield, Kathleen Norris, Henri Nouwen, and others fly off the shelves by the thousands. Even more telling is the response of readers, as experienced by Norris when more than three thousand people wrote to her, wanting to share their reactions to her books *Dakota* and *Cloister Walk*. Among evangelicals, the publishing frenzy surrounding books on spirituality is apparent as well. Books by Eugene Peterson, Dallas Willard, Philip Yancey, Richard Foster, and J. I. Packer have appealed to readers who desire to take their spiritual life to a deeper level. *Christianity Today* recently selected Willard's *Divine Conspiracy* as its book of the year. Also consider the recent sale of more than three million copies of *Chant,* the CD by the Benedictine Monks of Santo Domingo de Silos.

In some ways, it is ironic that on the heels of the "God is dead" movement and the powerful secularizing tide that followed it, threatening to remove religion from the rooms and corridors of every public edifice, this robust religious

> The search for what it means to be spiritual is the story, not just of the decade, but of the century.
>
> **Bill Moyers,** *Dallas Morning News*

quest has emerged—and not only endures but gathers momentum. It is interesting to note that Harvey Cox, reflecting on his *Secular City,* which was supposed to be a theological accommodation to the post-religious age, has conceded that we are experiencing instead "a period of renewed religious vitality, another 'Great Awakening'" and wonders how the predictors could have been so wrong.[3]

I still recall some of my undergraduate professors who went to great lengths to make sure no one believed in biblical truths anymore. That may have something to do with the cause of the inextinguishable spiritual blaze sweeping our country. Charles Knuckles of Emory University has suggested, "We've stripped away what our ancestors saw as essential—the importance of religion and family. . . . People feel as if they want something they've lost, but it has left a gaping hole."[4] However surprising it may be to bystanders, this soaring interest in spirituality is undeniably real and gaining momentum. It is here and will not go away. It has become a force, influencing pastors, congregations, denominations, and seminaries.

This vigorous spiritual impetus is also sprouting outside the confines of Christianity. Mickey Singer, the wealthy CEO of Medical Manager, personifies this non-Christian spirituality. His pilgrimage began a few years ago when he read *Autobiography of a Yogi* and, as a consequence, decided to practice meditation, leading to what he described as a deep spiritual awakening.

He then began to teach spirituality at the nearby Santa Fe Community College. Eventually his research and teaching coalesced into a book, *The Search for Truth*. Through his teaching and writing he developed a small following, and he began meeting with his followers regularly for meditation. Now a group of fifty gathers weekly in the "Temple of the Universe" built on Singer's property. Their syncretistic services include meditation, music, and a "Mickey talk" on living the spiritual life.[5]

Indiscriminate Spiritual Seekers

One disturbing problem with this spiritual hunger—as is often true of voracious physical hunger—is that it is undiscerning. This may result from a widespread ignorance of the Bible and Christianity, as well as popular misperceptions, especially of evangelical Christianity. This lack of discernment may also be attributable to the rapid proliferation of denominations and churches accompanied by a pervasive erosion of denominational loyalty and an unawareness of and lack of interest in our Christian heritage. A general rootlessness often marks the evangelical world. Though one foot is solidly planted on Scripture, the other is perched on relevance. Often in its rush to adapt to the contemporary, the church has unconsciously snipped ties to its rich heritage.

In some instances, people with strong spiritual interests who have experienced disappointment and disillusionment with a church or denomination have sought satisfaction elsewhere—that is, somewhere other than in Christianity. There is no doubt that millions of seekers and believers have been alienated from Christianity in one way or another, but not because they lack an interest in spiritual matters. As someone said to me, "I am committed to

> The Christian life and true spirituality are not to be seen as outward at all, but inward.
>
> Francis Schaeffer, *True Spirituality*

God but turned off by the local church." William Hendricks also pointed this out in his book *Exit Interviews*, observing that many Christians who have left the church because they have been hurt or disillusioned want to remain Christians and to grow spiritually.[6] In spite of everything, they are still seeking the Lord.

Robert Wuthnow, in his scintillating new book, *After Heaven: Spirituality in America Since the 1950s*, argues that there has been a transition from seeking spirituality in sacred places to a new spirituality of seeking knowledge and practiced wisdom through glimpses of the sacred. The movement is from a spirituality of place to a spirituality of seeking. His analysis offers new insight into the multidirectional nature of current spiritual stirrings.

Historical perspective underscores the importance of these developments. At the start of the twentieth century, virtually all Americans practiced their faith within a Christian or Jewish framework. They were cradle-to-grave members of their particular traditions, and their spirituality prompted them to attend services and to believe in the teachings of their churches and synagogues. Organized religion dominated their experience of spirituality, especially when it was reinforced by ethnic loyalties and when it was expressed in family rituals. Even at mid-century, when the religious revival of the 1950s brought millions of new members to local congregations, many of these patterns prevailed. Now, at the end of the twentieth century,

15

growing numbers of Americans piece together their faith like a patchwork quilt. Spirituality has become a vastly complex quest in which each person seeks in his or her own way.[7]

The dominant American automobile manufacturers in some ways exemplify what has happened in American churches. Unresponsive to consumer demand while stubbornly designing and churning out models they thought the car owner would buy, they watched their market share steadily erode. At one time Cadillac was the overwhelming first choice for affluent Americans, but not anymore. Mercedes, Lexus, and BMW now dominate this market. Ford and Chevrolet were once the preferred cars for middle-class Americans; now the Toyota Camry and Honda Civic are near the top of the list, if not at the top.

In similar fashion, millions of churchgoers who became turned off by their experiences dropped out. The old mainline denominations, failing to respond, lost countless numbers of members and eventually their dominance. Some churchgoers, of course, gravitated to other kinds of churches and ministries, especially evangelical alternatives, but often such moves left them disappointed and disillusioned once again. Rebuffed, told they don't know what they are talking about or that what they are seeking doesn't exist, they have been offered unsatisfactory substitutes and, in the process, have been bruised by the resistant, insensitive side of the church.

Some Catholics became Protestants; some Protestants became Catholics. Some dropped out of church entirely, never to return. Some of the dropouts sought or are seeking religious alternatives to Christianity. In fact, their numbers have increased dramatically in recent years. Unfortunately, the church seems unmindful or unconcerned that many of these seekers are not even considering Christianity. These seekers have "been there, done that." Unless something changes, they may become permanently lost to Christianity.

Richard Lovelace clearly identified the problem twenty years ago in *The Dynamics of Spiritual Life:*

> Spirituality is in many ways treated as the neglected stepchild of the Christian movement. It is often reduced to an emotional frosting spread over the surface of the other parts of Christianity which are considered more substantial and important, such as the maintenance of sound doctrine, correct social engagement or institutional policy. But it is seldom recognized to be the indispensable foundation without which all of these are powerless and fall into decay. In parts of the church a fairly shallow spirituality is the bread and butter of daily experience, but it is almost invisible as a matter of serious concern among church leaders because it is either taken for granted or unconsciously held in contempt. . . . Other sectors have neglected a program of spiritual development because they have concluded that it is either too hard or not worth doing. In many of these circles spiritual theology, if its existence is recognized at all, is likely to be dismissed as "mere pietism."[8]

A Window of Opportunity

Nonetheless, though the current religious stirring may be marked more by dabbling than depth, it is a major phenomenon not to be ignored, for it offers the greatest opportunity in decades for a genuine spiritual renewal and awakening. If the Christian church is sensitive to this opportunity and marshals its energies to respond to the apparent activity of God's Spirit, who knows what might happen. There is every possibility of a spiritual resurgence that could radically change the way people think and live—as much as the immense and enduring influence of the Great

Awakening of the 1700s. The eminent author G. K. Chesterton, in describing this country as shaped by that spiritual movement, once referred to America as "a nation with the soul of a church." Though it no longer bears that distinct character, prominent in earlier centuries, it definitely contains a growing number of citizens who have developed a spiritual restlessness. This restlessness and searching in itself marks a new window of opportunity to share the gospel so that they may believe in Christ and begin to grow spiritually. If the Christian church seizes this grand window of opportunity and reaches large numbers of these spiritual seekers, the twenty-first century could become the Christian century that was anticipated at the beginning of the twentieth century. If that were to happen, it could change the spiritual landscape for the foreseeable future. What a way to begin the third millennium!

When Charles Sheldon wrote *In His Steps,* he envisioned how the world might become different were people to ask, "What would Jesus do?" and order their lives accordingly. Perhaps we might do well to ask how the world would look if there were a great spiritual awakening at the beginning of the twenty-first century. Would people be more hopeful or pessimistic, cheerful or hostile? Would people be smiling and cooperative? Would the streets be cleaner and more handsomely landscaped? Would the air be cleaner and purer, the water fresher and safer? Would you need to lock your doors and engage security alarms? Would crime be minimized? What would the programming look like on television? How would movies be different? What moral standards would prevail? Would marriages become stronger, happier, and more durable? How would children be raised? How different would they behave? What would the major issues and challenges of society be?

When Fletcher Christian and his mutineers landed the *Bounty* off Pitcairn Island in 1790, they had an opportunity to make a new life for themselves. Though they got off to a good start, unfortunately things turned sour, and

> True spirituality is not a superhuman religiosity; it is simply true humanity released from bondage to sin and renewed by the Holy Spirit. This is given to us as we grasp by faith the full content of Christ's redemptive work; freedom from the guilt and power of sin.
>
> Richard E. Lovelace, *Dynamics of Spiritual Life*

eventually poisoned relationships degenerated into mass murder. Finally, all of the men, except for John Adams, were dead. He began reading the Bible to the children and teaching them hymns. Then something happened. The Spirit of God changed his heart, and eventually the children and women were converted also, so that by the time an English ship discovered them some years later in 1808, a model Christian community had emerged.

Why couldn't something on this order occur again on a larger scale? It certainly would not be the first time it has happened, as history powerfully reminds us. Consider the rise of the Christian church during the centuries immediately after Christ, the colossal impact of the Reformation, or the spiritual renewals of the eighteenth century in Europe and America.

As you may recall, when Alexis de Toqueville visited the United States in the early 1800s, he remarked on how different this country was from Europe. He enthusiastically commended the good he found and was especially impressed to see how many Americans were involved in one voluntary association or another for the purpose of doing good. He was struck by the Christian commitment that drove their activities. Now, approximately two hundred years later we need to experience afresh the powerful positive influence of spiritual renewal as it benefits and transforms both the individual and society as a whole. Taking a few moments to dream of what might be stimulates us to pray that much harder for such a spiritual movement to occur and for the current resurgence of spiritual stirrings to fasten themselves to the power of the gospel. Doesn't it make you want to do something—to work and pray for that to happen?

The Disciplines of the Spirit

In recent years the booming interest in spiritual matters, in addition to the spate of books and flood of music, has found two foci: (1) renewed awareness of and an interest in the spiritual disciplines, and (2) a new emphasis on two of those disciplines in particular: prayer and fasting.

In 1994, Bill Bright enthusiastically described for me his recent forty-day fast that he said had changed his life. He was so gripped by God's grace during that time that he sensed God's readiness to send a great spiritual awakening upon America, an awakening that was, in his opinion, desperately needed. Moreover, he explained how he was so motivated and transformed by his experience that he now wanted to encourage others to do the same. He invited many church leaders to join him in Orlando, Florida, in December 1994, for a time of prayer and fasting. Given the short notice, it is remarkable that nearly seven hundred people came. The response was extremely positive.

As a result, Campus Crusade has sponsored an annual Fasting and Prayer Conference. Other evangelical ministries have sponsored similar events, including the National Association of Evangelicals, the National Religious Broadcasters, World Vision, Mission America, and individuals such as Jerry Falwell, who says that he has heard more about fasting during the last five years than the previous forty-three years of his ministry. According to *Christianity Today,* teens are now fasting in record numbers too.[9]

Kay Wilson of Arcadia, California, is among those who have been attracted to fasting. For the forty days prior to Easter 1998, she lived on fruits and vegetables in order to draw closer to God and to pray for a nationwide spiritual awakening. Later she said, "It was the most meaningful Holy Week I had ever experienced."[10] The flood of testimonies regarding the benefits of prayer and fasting indicate she has lots of company.

Richard Foster has been foremost among those who have generated an interest in what may be called the disciplines of the Spirit. In doing so, he trades on the ascetic

> As the deer pants for streams of water,
> so my soul pants for you, O God.
> My soul thirsts for God, for the living God.
> When can I go and meet with God?
>
> Psalm 42:1–2

tradition of the church, a tradition much more familiar to Catholics than Protestants. In the Catholic tradition, it was said that these exercises or practices made communication and union with God possible. They were designed to be experience oriented rather than speculative so that anyone who would commit to the practice of these disciplines would benefit spiritually.

The discipline of these spiritual exercises is often compared to a physical training regimen. Paul said, "Train yourselves to be godly" (1 Tim. 4:7). The idea clearly communicated by this imagery is that you must practice these disciplines regularly if you want to strengthen yourself spiritually, just as you must exercise regularly if you want to strengthen your body.

Foster argues that to try to compete athletically without training is almost certain to bring failure. Without training, you can try to compete, but your body will not be able to respond to the demands put upon it, no matter how determined you are or how hard you try. The failure to train assures a failure in any serious competition because you have not developed the capacity to respond as needed in a competitive situation. The solution is simple: develop a regimen of training so you will not fail. So Foster says, one trains to be prepared to compete.[11]

Foster describes the various spiritual disciplines as he understands them, noting that he does not offer an exhaustive list and is unaware of the existence of one. His list of disciplines, with definitions of each, is well worth including here because of his widespread influence:

> Inward disciplines, like meditation, prayer, fasting, and study activate our heart and mind toward the way of Christ. Meditation is the ability to hear God's voice and obey his word. Prayer is ongoing dialogue with the Father about what we and God are doing together. Fasting is the voluntary denial of an otherwise normal function for the sake of intense spiritual activity. Study is the process through which we bring the mind to conform to the order of whatever we are concentrating upon.
>
> Outward disciplines, like simplicity, solitude, and submission, cultivate our appetites toward the way of Christ. Simplicity is an inward reality of single-eyed focus on God that results in an outward lifestyle free from "cumber" as William Penn put it. Solitude involves creating an empty open space for God that undercuts all the false support systems we use to shore up our lives. Submission is the ability to lay down the everlasting burden of needing to get our own way.
>
> Corporate disciplines, like confession, guidance, and celebration cultivate our affections toward the way of Christ. Confession is the grace through which the sins and

sorrows of the past are forgiven. Guidance is the experience of knowing the theocratic rule of Christ over our lives. Celebration is being as Augustine said, "an alleluia from head to foot."[12]

These disciplines, Foster is quick to add, have no merit in and of themselves, for we become acceptable to God "by grace alone, and our justification is by grace alone."[13] The point of such spiritual practices should not be to elevate these particular activities over the rest of life but "to electrify the spiritual impulse that animates all of life."[14]

Doing Something Spiritual

Foster's disavowal, however, may not be so clearly grasped by the new advocates and practitioners of these disciplines. For some people, these disciplines have merit in themselves and have become a means of achieving God's favor, perhaps to be used as leverage to achieve certain results such as revival. For others, it is doubtlessly nothing more than riding the crest of another fad. Such attitudes, however, in no way diminish the fact that these ancient spiritual disciplines, recently rediscovered by Protestants, may be of considerable benefit spiritually. In many instances they help people develop a focused emphasis on the inner life, on the all-important relationship with God.

The newfound interest in and practice of these disciplines by many Protestants is doubtless another sign of the current spiritual stirrings that are in evidence today. It is also evidence of a search for a spiritual reality that will work. Since other experiences and practices have failed to deliver, people think, why not try these spiritual disciplines? The fact that the disciplines are associated with a historic Christian tradition, a mystical spirituality, also lends appeal. People are able to maintain their Christian identity while capitalizing on their desire for an experiential spirituality.

Rather than reading another book about spirituality or repeating past experiences that proved unprofitable, those who are searching for spiritual authenticity want to take positive steps toward experiencing it. Spiritual disciplines, combined with an emphasis on the inner life, have great appeal to many Christians, for they offer a way to skirt legalism, formalism, intellectualism, and other isms that have generated emotional, psychological, and political turmoil within Christendom.

In some respects, the current spiritual interest with its varied manifestations is reminiscent of Daniel's era. Following the deaths of Nebuchadnezzar and his son Belshazzar, Darius the Mede came to power. Key administrators plotted against Daniel to keep the king from appointing him second in command. Asking for a law prohibiting prayer—except to the king—for thirty days, they used the

---

Everybody thinks of changing humanity and nobody thinks of changing himself.

Leo Tolstoy, *My Religion*

---

king's vanity to lay a trap for Daniel, since they were sure he would continue to pray to God in spite of the new law. They were right and succeeded in having Daniel thrown into the lions' den as his punishment for breaking the recently enacted law. Darius was terribly distressed, but he was bound by his word. Following a sleepless night, he hurried to the door of the lions' den at the first light of day. Perched at the entrance of the den he yelled, "Daniel, did your God save you?" He was anxious to know if Daniel was alive, but he was asking a bigger question as well. Deep down he wanted to know if God was real and if he could make a difference in Daniel's life (Dan. 6:20).

People everywhere, in all stages of life, are asking, "Is God real? Can he make a difference in my life? If so, how can I relate to him positively?" They have begun to realize that the vertical dimension of their lives is void, and they want to reestablish it by seeking spiritual authenticity. If God is real, he can make a difference—*the* difference—and they want to connect with him.

The pages that follow describe in brief fashion the kind of difference God can and should make in the life of one who connects to him spiritually and begins the journey toward spiritual maturity. Hopefully, this overview will whet your appetite so you will continue to learn and grow spiritually, pleasing and honoring God by the kind of person you become.

QUESTIONS FOR REFLECTION

1. Are you aware of new spiritual expressions in your region? List them. How would you evaluate these diverse stirrings?
2. What is the cause of spiritual stirrings? What Scripture verses fit your answer?
3. How important is the search for spirituality? Why?
4. What lessons can be learned from the church's mistakes regarding spirituality?

CHAPTER TWO

GODLINESS AND SPIRITUAL MATURITY

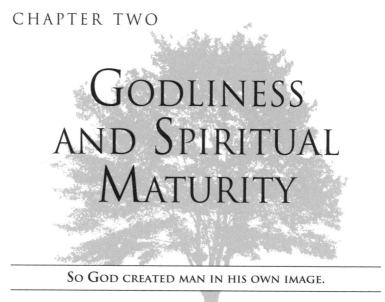

SO GOD CREATED MAN IN HIS OWN IMAGE.

GENESIS 1:27

After the usual perfunctory greetings following the funeral service, Alice and Robert were walking to their car in the parking lot when Alice said, "I'm going to miss Helen. She was the finest Christian I have ever known."

You may have heard similar statements on occasion, but they raise the question, How do we know who is a fine Christian and who is not? To phrase it another way, How do you become a person of spiritual stature? How do you attain spiritual maturity? How would you know if you or someone else has attained spiritual maturity? If you were asked to survey the membership of a local congregation to determine who is spiritually mature, what identifying

26

marks would you look for? Can you compile a list of characteristics that would enable you, with some confidence, to recognize spiritual maturity when you encounter it?

I have often asked these questions, listening carefully to the replies. They usually involve Bible reading, prayer, and church activity or ministry. For example, some might say a strong or spiritually mature Christian is someone who reads the Bible regularly, someone who is a serious Bible student, or someone who really knows the Bible. Others may point to people who pray sincerely and devoutly to God, real prayer warriors, or perhaps people who know how to talk to God. It is not unusual to view prayer and meditation on Scripture as the epitome of a devotional life that reaches the highest levels of divine approval. Nor is it unusual for someone to suggest that intense involvement in the life of the church or a Christian ministry is a defining factor. Unfortunately, this is tantamount to making frequency of attendance or level of activity or status in the church the determining criteria of spiritual maturity.

There is, of course, good reason for people to suggest these answers or they would not be offered so often. After all, people respond, why would you engage in such activities unless you were a Christian, and a serious one at that? How else can you justify the motivation? As activity level increases, you would usually expect it to signal a deepened commitment or higher level of spiritual attainment, wouldn't you? Following this line of thought, it is perfectly plausible to expect ministers, missionaries, church officers and leaders to be at a comparably higher level of spiritual development than other Christians.

The Means of Grace and Spiritual Maturity

Yet, however reasonable this may seem, it does not always work this way and is definitely not the way to assess spiritual growth. This may come as a surprise, but the fact is you may do all of these things—read the Bible daily or read through the Bible yearly, pray frequently and fervently, and be extremely active in a congregation or Christian organization—without even being a Christian, much less a spiritually mature Christian. It happens.

Think about it! The devil knows the Scriptures, doesn't he? Satan did not hesitate to quote the Bible when tempting Christ (Matt. 4:1–10). Unbelievers have been and still are biblical scholars. They may be accomplished academicians or widely published authors. That is not unusual. The Jesus Seminar of the '90s certainly seems to qualify. The Pharisees of Jesus' day, though their hearts were far

> When God created man, he made him in the likeness of God. He created them male and female and blessed them. And when they were created, he called them "man."
>
> **Genesis 5:1–2**

from the Lord, set an enviable example of disciplined devotion and dogged, compulsive obedience to the law according to their interpretation of it. In their world, if you had asked the average Jewish citizen on the street who would most likely get to heaven, the answer would have been a Pharisee or a Sadducee.

To counter that kind of thinking, as you may recall, Jesus sternly warned that not all who pray "Lord, Lord" will enter the kingdom of heaven. He cautioned his listeners not to make false assumptions about their spiritual status or future spiritual reward, for although they could point to things they had done in his name, such as prophesying, casting out demons, and performing miracles, they might still hear the judgment, "I never knew you. Away from me" (Matt. 7:21–23).

The message is clear. You should be careful about the criteria you choose for assessing the assurance of your salvation or spiritual maturity. Regardless of popular opinion, it is a mistake to assume that prayer, study of the Bible, and active participation in worship or ministry guarantee you or anyone else spiritual status, since they do not even guarantee faith. Why is this so?

The basic error is often one of confusing the methods or means of spiritual growth with the marks of spiritual maturity. The phrase "means of grace" has been used through the years to refer to the medium through which grace may be received. The means of grace for strengthening the faith of the Christian are generally understood to be the Word of God, sacraments, and prayer. Once you become a Christian, they become the primary channel by which you draw closer to God and grow spiritually. Reading God's Word and hearing it preached or taught, regularly joining in public worship at a church, receiving the sacraments, and participating in prayer and support groups are foundational to one's growth and development in Christ. They do not, however, automatically guarantee spiritual growth, as noted above. Rather, they must be received sincerely in faith and with gratitude or they may become the means of condemnation and judgment for the believer (John 12:47–48; 1 Cor. 11:29). That is why these activities should be understood as *means of grace* for spiritual growth not the *actual marks* of spiritual maturity. They are the vehicles to help you reach spiritual maturity but must not be equated with it.

The Image of God and Spiritual Maturity

The question remains, How can you discern those who have approached spiritual maturity in contrast to those who are just beginning the journey of faith? Are you spiritually mature? Immature? What criteria or characteristics point to spiritual maturity? One response might be, look for the fruit of the Spirit as described by Paul in Galatians 5:22–23:

love
joy
peace
patience
kindness
goodness
faithfulness
gentleness
self-control

This makes sense because these qualities are a sign of spirituality, marking the presence and influence of the Holy Spirit, who brings them to fruition. However, the most satisfactory and straightforward answer to this question is that God wants you to become like him, conformed to his image in Christ (Rom. 8:29; Eph. 4:23–24). This is what God intends for your spiritual pilgrimage.

Let's consider why this is true and what it means to be conformed to God's image. To do so drives us back to the first pages of the Bible. There we read that Adam and Eve were created in God's image at the dawn of the universe (Gen. 1:27). They were like him and enjoyed an intimate relationship with him. That image was soon marred or distorted, however, by their sinful disobedience. This disobedience alienated them from God, resulting in tension if not outright hostility with God, dramatically portrayed by their banishment from the Garden of Eden.

The placement of the cherubim at the gate of the Garden, brandishing a flaming sword to bar Adam and Eve from returning, was an unmistakable mark of God's judgment. Their sinful folly had cost them their unique role in paradise, along with all its benefits. The nobility of the human race was severely eroded, resulting in a dehumanizing trend that would eventually lead to all kinds of inhuman acts. Moreover, they would not be able to re-enter the Garden and regain what had been lost. That now was impossible. There would have to be another solution.

The gospel is the solution God provides to all who are under his judgment. Everyone must repent of the sin that has estranged him or her from God and trust in Christ for forgiveness and acceptance. The gospel is a message of

> We now begin to bear the image of Christ, and we are daily being transformed into it more and more; but that image depends upon spiritual regeneration. But then, it will be restored to fullness, in our body as well as our soul: what has now begun will be brought to completion, and we will obtain in reality what as yet we are only hoping for.
>
> John Calvin, *Calvin's Commentaries*

hope, but it is also a message of transformation, because all who genuinely repent and believe are changed forever. They are born again spiritually. The old person is left behind and the new person takes over. When people become Christians, they do so as spiritual babies who begin a process of spiritual growth. The nature of the change following conversion is an experience of grace that gradually remakes believers so that they become more and more like God. That is what spiritual growth means—being remade into the image of God. It is a progressive experience of conformity to the character of God.

Now, let me be crystal clear. Scripture does not say that believers become gods or God. Though some movements teach or have taught this, that is not what the Bible teaches. As a matter of fact, Satan's temptation of Adam

31

and Eve may have contained an element of this false teaching. He seemed to say, "God doesn't want you to eat this fruit because then you will be on the same level with him, knowing good and evil" (see Gen. 3:1–5). "Why should God be the only one to have such knowledge? It isn't fair of him to keep it from you. He must be selfishly trying to keep it all for himself. But you can have it too." Being created by God never assured Adam and Eve, nor has it assured any other human, the same status as God. We are accountable to him, not equal with him, and that accountability is endemic to the very nature of the creature as distinct from the Creator.

But to become *like* God is an entirely different matter and greatly to be desired. Paul, in fact, urges believers to become imitators of God as his dearly loved children (Eph. 5:1). Children consciously and unconsciously assume the vocabulary and mannerisms of their parents, whom they love and esteem. Similarly, we should want to be more like our Father in heaven.

The terms often used to describe Christian faith or behavior reflect this idea of becoming more like God. For example, the word *godly* is commonly used to refer to someone who is so spiritual he or she reminds you of God. To say that someone is spiritual is a reference to the influence or presence of the Holy Spirit in his or her life. To be Christlike is to reflect the person of Christ. To be conformed to God's image is to reflect his character or attributes in thought and behavior. The attributes of God should become more and more apparent until they reach a well-defined expression in the mature Christian.

The Attributes of God

If believers are to be conformed more and more to the attributes of God, then it is imperative to identify these attributes so that we know what God expects. We cannot know who we are or what we should be until we truly know God. This means we must discover what God is like and how he has revealed himself to us.

The most important step any person can take toward spiritual growth is to seek a better knowledge of God. The response of thousands of Christians to the publication of J. I. Packer's *Knowing God* was a popular demonstration of this fact. In this light, it is easy to understand the emphasis the reformers placed on gaining a knowledge of God. John Calvin began his monumental *Institutes of the Christian Religion* by discussing this topic.

> Now, the knowledge of God, as I understand it, is that by which we not only conceive that there is God but also grasp what befits us and is proper to his glory, what is to our advantage to know of him. . . . Moreover, although our mind cannot apprehend God without rendering some honor to him, it will not suffice simply to hold that there is One whom we all ought to honor and adore, unless we are also persuaded that he is the fountain of every good, and that we must seek nothing elsewhere than in him. . . . For until men recognize that they owe everything to God, that they are nourished by his fatherly care, that he is the Author of their every good, that they should seek nothing beyond him—they will never yield him willing service.[1]

In his Geneva Catechism, published in 1537, Calvin made it plain that the purpose of life is to know God. In it he defined piety, or what we might refer to as spirituality:

> True piety does not consist in a fear which willingly indeed flees God's judgment, but since it cannot escape is terrified. True piety consists rather in a sincere feeling which loves God as Father as much as it fears and reverences Him as Lord, embraces His righteousness, and dreads offending Him worse than death. And whoever has been endowed

with this piety dare not fashion out of their own rashness any God for themselves. Rather, they seek from Him the knowledge of the true God and conceive Him just as He shows and declares Himself to be.[2]

God has revealed himself to us most clearly through Scripture. He has also revealed himself to us through the universe, his creation, and through other Christians. In biblical times he revealed himself through unusual appearances, such as the angel of the Lord or the pillar of fire. All of these sources of information are helpful to us in coming to know God, but Scripture provides the only infallible record and guide. Moreover, Scripture is our source for the knowledge of God as Savior.

Gathering this information and seeking to understand it, as well as use it to interpret our experience, enable us to have a true and accurate understanding of who God is and what he is like, although such knowledge is far from exhaustive. Further, even with all the information available, what person could claim to know God completely or comprehensively? The important thing is that we know him truly.

As we learn more about God, we discover characteristics or attributes that, when grouped together, give us a mental picture of him. These attributes constitute his nature and are essential to his existence. Without these attributes, God would not exist. Some of God's attributes are communicable (transmittable) and others are incommunicable (incapable of being imparted). For example, God is infinite and unchanging. We cannot and will not become like God in this respect; these qualities are true only of God. These are incommunicable attributes that we will not experience as a consequence of spiritual transformation.

However, we will be able to experience other attributes (communicable attributes) to varying degrees, such as the wisdom, love, and goodness of God. These qualities were severely damaged due to the fall, resulting in the distortion of God's image in humankind. Now, however, through God's work of salvation that remakes us into his image, these characteristics are being renewed in us.

Changed Lives

Spiritual growth is transformation. Lives are changed from those of unbelief to belief, from ungodliness to godliness. Although our transformation will not be complete until the glory of heaven is realized, a recognizable change begins with conversion and continues throughout life. Life may have ups and downs, spurts of great growth and slower times of imperceptible advance, but it is a new and different life empowered and directed by the Holy Spirit. What we were becomes more and more distant and different from

> **Men don't know that they are godly by believing that they are godly.**
>
> **Solomon Stoddard,** *Guide to Christ*

the new person who is becoming more and more like the Lord we have come to love. It is somewhat reminiscent of photographs taken during various phases of life. The progression from infancy to childhood to youth and then on to the stages of adulthood reveals striking changes. Spiritual growth involves a similar progression, and every day God's attributes should be more clearly apparent and enduring in us. That is the mark of spiritual growth.

Consider the Sermon on the Mount in this light (Matt. 5:1–7:29). Jesus began his great sermon with a surprising statement regarding the poor in spirit, or "the beggars of the spirit." He might well have said, "The best thing that can happen to you is to acknowledge your spiritual impoverishment. You are spiritually destitute, so the road to happiness begins when you admit you are sinful through and through. Everything you think and touch is in some way tainted by sin. It pervades and corrupts your entire life, holding you captive like an addiction. But of greater concern is that it brings you under the wrath and judgment of the holy God, who cannot have fellowship with sin. Do you realize that the consequence of your sinfulness means eternal punishment? If so, then you have taken the first step toward true happiness." This is similar to John's assertion that "if we claim to be without sin, we deceive ourselves and the truth is not in us" (1 John 1:8). The first step toward deliverance is to admit we have a problem, which opens the door of receptivity to change. Jesus, therefore, forcefully emphasized the problem before proceeding.

After obtaining the undivided attention of his listeners with this striking opening, Jesus continued. "Once you recognize the magnitude of your problem, the best thing you can do is repent—mourn because of the sin that has separated you from God, triggered his anger, and brought you under his judgment. If you genuinely grieve for the way you have spoiled your life and offended God, there is hope. If you are distressed because of the harm you have done and are therefore willing to reject this way of life, you can begin anew, finding peace and comfort. If you hunger and thirst for the righteousness that comes from above—from the Lord—and can be received through faith in the Savior he has promised, then there is hope for you." Or as John put it, "If we confess our sins, he is faithful and just and will forgive us our sins and purify us from all unrighteousness" (1 John 1:9).

As you can see, Jesus' words parallel an evangelistic conversation in which you might say to someone, "You have failed to meet the expectations of your Creator, who will someday require you to give an account for your life. He calls your failure 'sin' and says that because of your sin you are squarely under his judgment. You face eternal punishment. Once the sentence is pronounced, it cannot be reversed; there will be no second chance. This is bad news, but it is true. Your only hope is to repent of your sins before it is too late and plead for his forgiveness through faith in Christ, who suffered the punishment your sins deserve when he died on the cross."

The initial comments of the Sermon on the Mount can be viewed as an abbreviated presentation of the gospel, explaining how these curious listeners could become believers, or children of God. Once Jesus had done that, he began to describe what a child of God looks like so they would understand the difference it would make in their lives if they believed. When you are a part of God's family, you are merciful, pure in heart, and a peacemaker, Jesus explained. With these succinct words, Jesus described the happy or blessed person who belongs to the Father's family.

It is important to note how each of the characteristics mentioned in his brief description finds its origin in the being of God. Having received forgiveness from the one who is the fountainhead of mercy, Jesus says, the child of God learns to be merciful and forgiving also (Eph. 4:32; cf. Matt. 18:21–35). What is more characteristic of true Christianity than the capacity to forgive, mirroring the God of grace who is so rich in mercy? It also reminds us of Jesus himself, who, experiencing the agony of crucifixion, looked at those who had done this to him and prayed, "Father, forgive them, for they do not know what they are doing" (Luke 23:34).

A reference to the pure in heart reminds us that a love for what is virtuous, righteous, and just should also mark believers because they belong to the holy God of truth and righteousness. His holiness should motivate them to embrace purity and reject all immorality. As they do so, they will point others to his perfect goodness.

God's children will also be peacemakers not trouble-makers, because God is the author of peace. His only begotten Son holds the title "Prince of Peace" (Isa. 9:6; John 14:27). Through their advocacy of peace, believers will discover in Christ a peace that unbelievers will never know. Though the world is full of troublemakers who stir things up and sow strife, those who follow God's way turn swords into plows and pour oil on troubled waters, bringing peace. The result of their peaceable ways is harmony and cooperation, usually in strong, durable relationships. Theirs is a path of reconciliation rather than estrangement.

If you want the character of God to characterize you, you will want to compile a list of God's attributes and then seek to discover how they can come to expression in your life. For the purpose of this book, we do not need to examine every attribute. We will, however, consider five, using them as examples: love, holiness, wisdom, sovereignty, and creativity.

The Cost of Changed Lives

Those whose lives are changed to conform to God's attributes may discover, according to Jesus, that they will be misunderstood, misrepresented, and maligned—perhaps even persecuted. That should come as no surprise since the prophets who came before were also persecuted (Matt. 5:11–12). Certainly Christ was persecuted, as were the apostles. It has not been unusual for the Lord's people, because of their different approach to life, to be resented by those who do not share the same convictions. In Oxford, England, you can still observe the prominent marker, referred to as the "Martyrs Memorial," standing as a reminder of Thomas Cranmer, Nicholas Ridley, and Hugh Latimer, who were burned to death because they refused to recant their confessions of faith. Throughout the centuries, thousands of Christians have suffered—even been martyred—because of their identity with Christ. Such persecution continues today in parts of the world. Hundreds of thousands of believers have been martyred in recent years, perhaps more in this century than all prior centuries combined.[3] It could happen to you some day if you resolutely stand for that which is godly.

Regardless of the ridicule or rejection a believer endures, there is a positive result: an assurance that the changed

> This conformity of nature between God and man is not only the distinguishing prerogative of humanity, so far as earthly creatures are concerned, but it is also the necessary condition of our capacity to know God, and therefore the foundation of our religious nature.
>
> Charles Hodge, *Systematic Theology*

life of a Christian will have an influence for good. God will use a believer's life like salt and light, a positive influence on an unbelieving world. As unbelievers observe the good deeds that represent lives transformed by God's grace, they become aware of God's existence and influence (Matt. 5:13–16). In this way, God is glorified through the lives of his people as his attributes come to expression in them, and other people begin to realize not only that God exists but also what he is like. They are drawn to him as they realize who he is.

As much as we might wish it otherwise, however, not everyone is drawn to God. Some resist him. With this in mind, we can appreciate the response of certain religious rulers and elders to Peter and John. Though the rulers and elders did not approve of these "unschooled, ordinary men," they quickly realized that Jesus had been a major influence on them (Acts 4:5–17). They detected clues in the behavior of Peter and John that clearly identified them with Jesus, and they saw that the apostles' preaching and teaching reflected a far greater understanding than would be expected of people with their background and education. Knowing Jesus clearly made a difference in the lives of the apostles.

Children of Light

In his letters, Paul addressed the difference that knowing Christ makes in the lives of believers. In Ephesians, he asserted that from eternity God had a plan to glorify himself by selecting a group of people whom he would love and make his own family, determining that their lives would be full of good works (Eph. 1:3–23; 2:6–10). Christians, therefore, should not live like unbelievers, Paul said, but in a way that is compatible with their new identity as part of God's family. Repudiating the behavior that is characteristic of the dark side of the life of unbelief, they need to "put on the new self, created to be like God in true righteousness and holiness" (Eph. 4:24). They must "be imitators of God, therefore, as dearly loved children" (Eph. 5:1) and children of light who are transparently different from the children of darkness (see Ephesians 4–6). Transformed lives that reveal the character of God are essential to God's mission in the world, issuing from his eternal purpose.

Given the biblical emphasis on changed lives, which should be radically different from those of non-Christians, it is disturbing to see so little difference between many church members and non-church members when it comes to moral and ethical standards. If our world were characterized by high standards of moral behavior, this fact might be somewhat more encouraging, but given the significant erosion of moral standards and behavior during the last forty years, this is a matter for serious concern.

Perhaps we have failed dramatically in our effort to teach people what God expects, and given the abysmal biblical ignorance that typifies the Christian populace, that may well be the case. You may wonder what is being accomplished by so many hours of Bible study and preaching. Perhaps many Christians do not care about being salt and light and find it easier and more desirable to accommodate their behavior to the unbelievers around them. Some may assume that only church-related matters should be influenced by faith. Perhaps many church members are not Christians but for one reason or another find it advantageous to be part of a church.

Whatever the reason for this lack of disparity in behavior, it is a serious problem. Christians should be different. If we are not developing a new way of thinking and living that is different from an unbelieving world, we cannot please God or hope to draw others to Christ. Something has to change. It is time for Christians to seriously consider how they live, especially if we are to take advantage of the spiritual stirrings in the land. If non-Christians see nothing distinctive about us, they will ask, "Why should we bother with Christianity? What difference does it make?"

Therefore, while the avenues to spiritual growth may be many, the destination of spiritual maturity is clearly and singularly understood as conformity to the image of God. When other people mingle with us and observe us in the ebb and flow of daily activities, they should be pointed to the Lord through transformed lives that reflect God's grace and character.

Character should be emphasized because spiritual growth involves the formation of character. Together, the characteristics of God reveal his character just as the various facets of our personalities, values, and behavior demonstrate our character. As your life is transformed by the Holy Spirit so that you become conformed more and more to the image of God, a character change is occurring in you. This character change, reflected in the transformation of your various characteristics or attributes, will make you more like the Lord and less like unbelieving people around you. From the inner core throughout, you will become different—a person of character, a godly person.

Don't let anyone convince you that character doesn't matter as long as you have faith—that as long as you believe, you can live however you wish. Real faith creates a new character as our lives are transformed to the characteristics of God. Such character formation shapes our behavior. When the heart is changed, the person changes. When enough people change, the culture changes, the world changes.

The following story from the early years of my ministry is indicative of how change can happen when we live and grow in Christ.

They Will See Your Good Works

John Berrios, a strikingly handsome teenager and the eldest of three children, was about to graduate from high school. Although his father was unable to work because of rheumatoid arthritis and the family existed on a meager income, John felt no obligation to help out. I thought he would want to help provide for his family's needs as soon as he could, but I was mistaken. Like most young men his age, adventure coursed through his veins. He wanted to get away from home and see the world, so he joined the Marines.

As his pastor, I sensed my responsibility to provide spiritual counsel. Knowing of his superficial interest in spiritual matters, made clear by minimal participation and a general lack of interest in church activities, our family invited him to a special going away dinner. At the very least, we also wanted him to know we cared about him. Afterward, John and I talked privately, and I took the opportunity to express my concern about his faith. I told him I hoped he would genuinely trust in Christ for his salvation and commit himself to live for the Lord. He thanked me for my concern but clearly rejected making a Christian commitment. As he put it, there were other things he preferred to do. So away he went to boot camp at Parris Island.

Following boot camp, John returned home briefly before shipping out to Vietnam. He stopped by my office to let me know he had changed his mind since our conversation and had decided to trust in Christ for his salvation. He seemed

> The entire world is a revelation of God, a mirror of his virtues and perfections; every creature is in his own way and according to his own measure an embodiment of a divine thought. But among all the creatures only man is in the image of God, the highest and richest revelation of God, and therefore head and crown of the entire creation.
>
> Herman Bavinck, *In the Beginning*

very happy about his decision. He did not say what had motivated his change of heart, but he wanted me to know of his new commitment. During the next few months, his letters from Vietnam expressed a true interest in spiritual matters and a growing desire to please the Lord.

Suddenly, eleven months after he left for Vietnam, while walking point on a patrol, John was shot by a sniper. Piercing the front of his body, the bullet tore a large hole in his back, severing his spinal cord and leaving him paralyzed from the waist down. After being rushed to a field hospital, his condition was stabilized. It soon became apparent, however, that he needed better care in order to survive, so he was flown to the Naval Hospital at Bethesda, Maryland.

There his parents and friends visited regularly as John's body responded to multiple surgeries and he fought to recover. By this time, however, the bronzed and muscular young Marine had wasted away to a shriveled frame of little more than one hundred pounds. He was tormented by bed sores the size of a fist, and he was confined to a room with an obnoxious person who made everyone around him miserable.

One day while John was sleeping, his mother started to tiptoe out for a cup of coffee. She had thought both fellows were sleeping, but John's roommate halted her and said, "I know what kind of person I am, but I have been watching John and listening to him talk about his faith. I know what he is like. The only thing I have to say is that his God must be a good God." John's mother did not know how to respond, so she merely nodded and left the room.

A few days later, at nineteen years of age, John Berrios went to live in heaven. Prior to that time, John's family had been nominally attached to the church—members but little more. Within weeks of John's death, however, his family was converted. First, his father changed into a spiritual dynamo who could not learn or do enough for the Lord. Then his mother and next his sisters came to love the God John had loved so much. Within a few months, more than thirty people associated with the family became Christians. Our church was never the same. Nor was I. Since that time, the observation "his God must be a good God" has been firmly fixed in my mind.

John's life changed. A child of God less than two years, he lived purposefully and joyfully for his Savior. Wherever he went, the difference was apparent. What a transformation occurred as the character of God shone through John. Many people were influenced and came to visit our church to learn more about the God in whom John believed. Through it all, God was glorified.

Few stories are so dramatic or influential, but God intends for all Christians to become so different, so much like him, that those who know us will exclaim, "Your God must be a good God." Jesus said, "Let your light shine

44

before men, that they may see your good deeds and praise your Father in heaven" (Matt. 5:16). That is what it means to be conformed to God's image.

QUESTIONS FOR REFLECTION

1. How should you evaluate spiritual maturity?
2. How are spiritual growth and maturity evaluated in your church?
3. Read the Sermon on the Mount (Matthew 5–7). How many of God's attributes are revealed in the sermon?
4. How is your life different from the lives of non-Christians you know?
5. How would you like to change?

CHAPTER THREE

The Love of the Triune God

... THAT THEY MAY BE ONE AS WE ARE ONE.

JOHN 17:22

Several years ago I was part of an audience that witnessed an emotional confession from two Christian parents who told us about a harrowing experience with their son. As a very young fellow, this son professed faith in Christ and seemed to be powerfully directed toward a missionary career. Following his education, for one reason or another, he was distracted from this calling and his interests wandered elsewhere. He moved to another city in order to take a job. Then, with the passage of time and the loss of contact with his parents and siblings, he began to do things that were incompatible with his family upbringing and his earlier Christian profession.

Finally, in awful turmoil, the young man phoned his brother to tell him how messed up his life had become and how he was now confronted by a new and unexpected problem—AIDS. He knew he did not have long to live. He needed help and there was nowhere else to turn. The brother listened as the young man described repeated efforts to find help at churches in his city. When those churches found out about his gay lifestyle, however, he became unwelcome. No one would help him. Church doors had been slammed shut.

Stunned by this new revelation, his brother asked, "Have you talked to Dad?" The young man replied, "No, I am not sure I can because I know how badly I have disappointed and hurt him." But then, at his brother's urging, the young man decided to call home and tell his father about his condition. With a halting voice, hardly knowing how or where to begin, he told his father how embarrassed and ashamed he was to admit what had happened. Once he began to talk, however, the story flowed like a river. Finally, when he had finished explaining everything, his father asked, "Son, do you remember the story of the prodigal?" The son replied, "Of course." His father said, "Like the father in the story, I am urging you to come home. We love you and we will help you."

As I listened to those parents pour out their hearts, I heard God's message of forgiveness and reconciliation in a fresh way. I became upset about our attitude toward those whom we may find repugnant, as evidenced by the church that shunned this young man who desperately sought help. The truth is that we are surrounded by people who have broken God's laws. We constantly encounter their pain, hurt, and alienation. Some of them are more unacceptable to us than others, but we must reach out and invite all of them to come home to the Savior, who offers forgiveness and reconciliation. They need to come home to begin healing and find a better life. When they do, we must not slam the door in their faces.

How do love, reconciliation, and forgiveness fit into God's pattern for our lives? Where is the source of such behavior and belief? We must begin with God to find the answers.

God Is Three in One

God is relational. He eternally exists in a relationship of intimacy and satisfaction, of unity and diversity. The loving, harmonious relationship that describes the three persons of the Trinity is no accident. Rather, it is expressive of the very essence of his nature. God exists in relationship and cannot be understood apart from it. He is one (Deut. 6:4), but he is also three as is clearly seen in the Great Commission (Matt. 28:19) and the apostolic benediction (2 Cor. 13:14). The Great Commission includes a mandate to baptize "in the name of the Father and of the Son and of the Holy Spirit." The apostolic benediction likewise links all three persons together in blessing.

Separate references to Christ, the Holy Spirit, and God the Father further emphasize God's triune nature—God is three and God is one. John leaves no doubt that the Word who became incarnate and lived among us was God (John 1:1–18). The high priestly prayer of Jesus recorded in John 17 is another example. As Jesus prayed for unity among believers, he did so on the basis of the unity of the Godhead, mentioning his relationship with the Father (John 17:20–26). Whatever else we may discover about God, there is no doubt that he is a relational being.

This truth of God's relationship within the Trinity dawned on me unexpectedly during a course on theology proper, or the doctrine of God, during my seminary years. My professor was explaining the first few verses of the

Gospel of John, verses I knew well, having already memorized them in English and Greek. He was primarily concerned about establishing the deity of Christ, as would be expected. I assumed that I knew exactly what he planned to say. Consequently, I was not listening as carefully as I should have when I was jolted to attention by his statement, "The Word was God's eternal fellow, bound to him as his companion forever."

Then my professor began to elaborate on a phrase I had completely ignored: "the Word was with God" (John 1:1). It had not seemed especially important to me, but he made it so by stressing the intimate relationship between Father and Son. I was chagrined to think of what I had overlooked

---

Could we with ink the ocean fill, and were the skies of parchment made,
Were every stalk on earth a quill, and every man a scribe by trade,
To write the love of God above would drain the ocean dry,
Nor could the scroll contain the whole though stretched from sky to sky.

Frederick Lehman, "The Love of God"

---

but excited by what I was beginning to grasp. The professor's eloquent discussion of the love that bound Father and Son together suddenly personalized God in a new way for me. I realized afresh that God is a personal God who feels and cares and loves—with a love that binds the Godhead and is extended to us.

I was reminded how easy it is to think of God in abstract, detached ways and how easily secular, non-biblical philosophies and experiences tend to shape our understanding of God. God is far different from Aristotle's pure thought or Aquinas's unmoved mover. Although many people may think of God much like "the force" of Star Wars or like a great monitor in the sky, he is quite different from an unknowable mysterious force out there somewhere. The Bible brings us face-to-face with a personal God who is throbbing with love, thriving on companionship—never an abstract, detached, impersonal being. When we meet this loving God who is relational through and through, we can finally understand why he created Adam and Eve.

Adam as a Relational Person

After God created Adam in his image, he said, "It is not good for the man to be alone. I will make a helper suitable for him" (Gen. 2:18). It is easy to read that statement without giving it a further thought. After all, it is nice to have company on occasion. But we might just as easily ask, What is wrong with being alone? Solitude, after all, can be a refreshing relief from the clamor and growing pressures of life. The point here is that it is not in Adam's nature to be alone permanently because he is, by virtue of being made in God's image, relational by nature—made for companionship and intimacy with God and with his own kind. Therefore, God gave Adam a craving for companionship with another human. Without that companionship, Adam found himself restless and incomplete.

Reread Genesis 1 and 2, and you will notice that this verse sticks out like a sore thumb in contrast to the litany of Genesis 1, in which after each successive stage of his creative work, God says, "It is good" (cf. Gen. 1:4, 10, 12, 18, 21, 25, 31). Hearing the repetitive refrain, "It is good, it is good, it is good," we are startled by the unexpected announcement in verse 2:18: "It is not good." From all that God has created, he singles out only one thing as unsatisfactory: Adam's aloneness. In doing so, God clearly emphasizes the relational nature of the one whom he made in his own image. Apart from this understanding, God's statement doesn't make sense. Given this explanation, the rationale—actually the necessity—for the creation of Eve is clearly established.

From the biblical account, we know that peace and harmony once ruled in the Garden of Eden, making it a place of idyllic beauty. What Adam and Eve experienced is beyond description; the Bible only hints at it, but it says enough to give us an idea. To think that they enjoyed such a unique fellowship with the Lord, walking with him in the Garden in the cool of the day, is beyond our capacity to comprehend completely. It appears as if there was a relationship of understanding with the animals, so that Adam innately knew the right names to give each one. Complete harmony existed in the lush, fertile Garden of Eden. What bliss!

Like it or not, we are relational creatures just like Adam and Eve. God has made us with an endemic desire to love and be loved because at the core of our being we are relational too. As John Donne wrote, "No man is an island." We cannot exist completely independent and separate from others.

From the moment of birth, in one way or another we discover our attachment to and need for others. Without the sharing of love and life, we are restless and incomplete. We yearn for satisfying and loving relationships. This is how we were created.

The Consequences of Disobedience

If that is true, then why is life so full of heartbreak, hostility, and estrangement? Obviously, something went wrong. We now know that things went awry when Adam and Eve disobeyed God and ate the one fruit he specifically told them not to eat (Gen. 2:16–17). That decision may have seemed trivial at the moment, but the results were cataclysmic, the extreme opposite of their expectations.

That one disobedient act shattered the harmony of their paradise, resulting in the immediate destruction of their relationship with God, their relationship with each other, and their relationship with the created world, including the animals. Stunned and ashamed, they hid from God, then turned on each other. The estrangement, tension, and hostility that followed were shocking new experiences. Too late, after they were banished from their idyllic setting, they began to realize what they had lost.

The consequences of their sin soon became all too evident when their son Cain murdered his brother Abel in cold blood (Gen. 4:8). It was a tragic moment in human

> In some sense the most benevolent generous person in the world seeks his own happiness in doing good to others, because he places his happiness in their good.
>
> Jonathan Edwards, *Charity and Its Fruits*

history when brother turned violently against brother. Looking back through the lens of Scripture, we now realize that alienation, estrangement, loneliness, and the various other forms of flawed and broken relationships that infect our lives find their origin in that first sin of Adam and Eve. Little did they realize what pain and misery they would inflict on all who came after them.

The rest of the Bible offers an unfolding commentary about the damage to human relationships that resulted from sin. The story of the Tower of Babel is a pertinent illustration. The tower was probably a ziggurat, with small steps up for people and big ones down for the deity. As such, it was a vain attempt to reach up to God and bring him down among the people through human effort. But the tower further compounded human estrangement from God and from one another, for when God came, he unexpectedly came in judgment—with terrible consequences (Gen. 11:1–9).

The movie *The Bible* captured it well by showing how friends and neighbors who were working together side by side on this great tower suddenly lost the ability to communicate with each other. They abruptly began to speak different languages and could no longer understand one another. Frustration due to their inability to communicate shifted quickly to suspicion and enmity. Fearful, they ran away from the tower and from one another, seeking safety and protection. Since that time, communication and community have been exasperatingly elusive, and human relationships have too often led to disillusionment and hurt. Think of Joseph and his brothers, David and Bathsheba, or the disciples of Jesus and the Pharisees. The pages of the Bible are replete with examples of relationship problems. Our own times provide no exception as the record of broken lives and wounded spirits continues unabated.

Why do people have trouble getting along? Why do they quarrel and fight? Why is human history strewn with the wreckage of war and stained with bloodshed? Why have racial groups hated and been hated? Why is there so much hurtful hostility?

Considering all the pain and trauma in human experience, it is easy to understand the statement, "The more I see of people, the more I like my dog." Yet, the hunger for companionship and intimacy remains regardless of disappointing experiences. As we create defensive strategies to cope with these hurts, the pressure mounts to find a satisfying relationship. Repression, self-deception, and other unhealthy reactions further complicate matters.

Sometimes our distorted drive for intimacy finds unusual expression, as in the case of homosexuality: the attraction of one male to another or one female to another. While it does underscore the essential relational nature of all people, homosexuality must be seen for what it is, a perversion of the normal desire for love and companionship. As such it reflects God's judgment against sin, forcefully noted by Paul in Romans 1:26–32. God's plan is for us to experience sexual intimacy and companionship in a marriage relationship between a man and a woman. With their children, husband and wife form a family, the basic unit of society.

As late as mid-century, who would have expected that at the close of the twentieth century the gay life would be condoned and openly promoted, even by Disney, the family entertainment leader? It underscores the distortion of our inner longings caused by sin. What is even more shocking is the acceptance of homosexuality by some sectors of American Christianity that sanction gay marriages and endorse the ordination of homosexuals. This is no isolated problem, rather a reflection of contemporary reality and its intrusive influence on the church. The collapse of external, moral, and legal restraints, coupled with the widespread loss of community, has certainly contributed to this development.

Sexual promiscuity, promoted in the media, has also failed to bring the happiness it promises. As the tragic stories of Marilyn Monroe, Elizabeth Taylor, and others remind us, neither multiple marriages nor multiple trysts assure intimacy. When you consider how frequently divorces now occur and how readily couples sleep together outside of marriage, sometimes in preference to marriage, you realize that true intimacy has been sacrificed on the altar of sexual gratification. The satisfaction of physical appetites does not yield intimacy. Rather, intimacy reveals that sexual gratification is a passionate expression of true oneness. The disappointment and disillusionment that come from failed marriages or brief affairs leave scars that are slow to heal. Meanwhile, the hurt and frustration that are a part of divorce often breed anger and alienation.

Sin has damaged relationships in many other ways. If anything, our modern era with large, energetic cities studded with a dazzling array of technology has resulted in a rapid disintegration of society. As you may recall, John Naisbitt in his *Megatrends* warned that high tech requires high touch.[1] We have more and more high tech with less and less high touch it seems. Strange, isn't it, that you can "reach out and touch someone" by phone or e-mail, yet it is more difficult than ever to connect personally. Relationships seem more fragile and the loss of community has become a colossal problem. Family solidarity has evaporated, replaced by fragile ties and more and more frequently by dysfunctionality. No wonder it has been said we are a nation of strangers. Cities breed anonymity as people get lost in the masses.

Crime grows like a weed fertilized by that anonymity. Its fruit is a new form of hostility—like the "road rage" that leads to violent acts among commuters or the anger that erupts into a shooting spree in a factory, fast-food franchise, or motel. In 1999 George Moody checked into the Johns Resort near Orlando, Florida, for a family reunion. When someone knocked on the door, he opened it. Three teens in ski masks opened fire leaving five wounded on the floor in pools of blood and debris. It was the last episode of a four-day shooting binge for the teens, who were seeking to create violence. But that bloody catastrophe was eclipsed by the massacre at Columbine High School in Colorado. Eric Harris and Dylan Klebold mercilessly gunned down twenty-nine students and faculty, killing thirteen. Shooting themselves as the authorities closed in, they abruptly ended their terrorizing rampage of hate.

Mutki, a teenager in Bangladesh, heard an intruder enter the room where she and her cousin Bina were sleeping. He had come with the intent of throwing acid over her in revenge for having his affections toward her rebuffed. Terribly scarred and disfigured—her face ruined, her eyesight destroyed—she will never be the same again. It is estimated that this kind of violence happened to two hundred women in India last year. Now Mutki, along with other victims, has become a social outcast, a fate worse than the grotesque physical disfigurement she endures.

In *Burned Out Case,* Graham Greene describes an architect of inestimable fame who leaves everything—money, prestige, friends, family—and travels to Africa, where his wanderings eventually lead him to a leper colony in a tiny village. He decides to stay for a while. The days pass as he becomes familiar with the grotesque and disfigured lepers whose eyes are red, bulging, and blind. The flesh on their noses has slowly rotted away, as have their hands, leaving stumps where there were once powerful fingers. Watching them come and go in their tattered rags, he realizes the disease has become so far advanced that they no longer feel. Reflecting on his experiences, especially the price of life, he concludes, "I am a burned out case just like these people." He spoke for too many in the modern world who have become like him—burned out with no feeling or compassion. Life for them has become mechanical and empty.

Reconciliation and the Gospel

What can be done about this problem? This is where the gospel is so compelling, for the first great effect of salvation is reconciliation to God and the immediate discovery of a refreshing fellowship with him. It is the recovery of a relationship that was lost through that first sin of Adam and Eve (cf. Rom. 5:12–21). When we speak of salvation, redemption, or eternal life, therefore, we cannot afford to ignore the term *reconciliation.* Paul uses it to describe the redemptive effort of the sinless Son of God, who took our sin on himself and in our place suffered the punishment we deserve so that we might receive the righteousness of God through him (2 Cor. 5:21). God was reconciling the world to himself in Christ, Paul said, not counting our sins against us but finding a way to forgive us and reconcile us to himself (2 Cor. 5:18–19). The gospel is the solution to the ruined relationships that sour our taste of life. Being remade in God's image means rebuilding relationships.

Scripture makes it plain that Christ, through his atoning death on the cross, removed the barriers that divide us from one another as well as from God. For our sake he was rejected and despised, ridiculed and scorned, imprisoned and beaten. He was forced outside the city walls and crucified. When he died—rejected, abandoned, and God-forsaken—he did this for us so that through our repentance and faith in him, the Father would accept us. If you believe in him and are reconciled to God, you join the beloved circle of those whose names are written in the Book of Life. Not only that, you can be sure that although he was cut off and forsaken, he has promised never to forsake you (Heb. 13:5). Because he was rejected, you are now accepted. You belong to him (John 10:27–30). You are family. There is a place for you at his table.

Reconciliation and Relationships

Reconciliation is horizontal as well as vertical; it affects our relationship with others. Paul, in his Letter to the Ephesians, used three powerful images to convey the comprehensive nature of God's reconciling work by which the uncircumcised and circumcised would through his grace become one. He referred to the three basic institutions of society—family, church, and state—speaking of these groups as fellow citizens, members of God's household, and a holy temple (Eph. 2:19–22). Unity in Christ transcends all of these.

Christ rips down the walls that divide us—culture, nationality, ethnicity, theology, denominations, gender—reconciling us to God and to each other. While nationality unites those within its boundaries, it tends to separate one citizenry from another, yet the grace of God in reconciliation enables us to transcend these human barriers. It enables me to find an immediate rapport and kinship

> The human mind is endowed with . . . an inborn need to hate and fight.
>
> George Simmel, *Sociology Soziologie*

with a believer in China, Korea, Africa, or any other place on earth. The basis for genuine ecumenicity is the sense of belonging that exists among believers. This community of faith transcends all earthly ties. It assures us that in Christ we are all brothers and sisters. The older I have become, the more it means as a Christian to enjoy fellowship with others who know Christ and the more I have begun to realize how unimportant our labels of denomination and theology will be in heaven compared to the oneness we have in Christ. So I am looking for more ways to recognize, celebrate, and promote this unity in Christ.

Relational reconciliation is integral to being remade in the image of God. Once our vertical relationship with God is restored, horizontal relationships with people must follow. Because we are new creatures in Christ, we are no longer able to regard others from a worldly point of view (2 Cor. 5:16). Therefore, we should develop a passion for reconciling others to God so that they may share our experience. We should also develop a passion for reconciling ourselves to others. Since we are all one through faith in Christ, we experience an innate desire, as part of his family, to repair relationships by reaching out to each other (Gal. 3:28–29). God is displeased when we erect walls to divide us from one another. The degree to which we cause any rift or division demonstrates a spiritual deficiency that should be acknowledged and corrected.

True Spirituality

Francis Schaeffer expressed it well, especially in *True Spirituality* and *Two Contents, Two Realities*. In the latter, he insisted that where true spirituality exists, there is "a beauty in human relationships." That assertion emanated from the crucible of his painful experience as a participant in the intense conflict within Presbyterianism early in the twentieth century. That conflict, in turn, was part of a broader fundamentalist-modernist controversy, a conflict that estranged believers from one another and resulted in the establishment of new denominations. Reflecting on this experience years later, Schaeffer acknowledged that although he and others of similar persuasion had a great concern for the truth, they did not have an equal concern for others. As a result, many well-intentioned believers who disagreed about how to deal with the issues at hand inflicted deep emotional and psychological wounds upon one another, leaving ugly scars and embittered stubborn alienation. The cumulative effect of the problems and conflict he encountered during this period and in the years following took its toll on Schaeffer, bringing him by 1951 to the brink of despair and abandonment of all he had fought to preserve. It was, in his own words, a time of "spiritual crisis."[2]

After several months of secluded prayer, Scripture reading, and contemplation, Schaeffer emerged with a new understanding of spirituality, one that rejected the ugly mean-spiritedness he had so often encountered. This true spirituality as he now understood it, apart from its resolute commitment to orthodoxy, was clothed in peace and harmony both in regard to human relationships and relationship with God. It would be like a soothing balm applied to the raw, mangled flesh of humanity.

Schaeffer was right. The brokenness of our wounded, bleeding world, a world fragmented by a traumatic loss of community and unable to heal itself, presents an extraordinary opportunity to demonstrate the power of the gospel. This can best be done by demonstrating reconciliation at work through repairing the damage and healing wounds. His advice to the Christian community, based on that experience, was,

> I plead with you, therefore, if, or when, that moment comes for you, that you find some way to show an observable love among *true* Christians before the world. Don't divide into ugly parties. If you do, the world will see an ugliness which will turn it off. Your children will see the ugliness, and you will lose some of your sons and daughters. They will hear such harsh things from your lips against men that they know have been your friends that they will turn away from you. Don't throw your children away, don't throw other people away by forgetting to observe, by God's grace, the principles simultaneously—to show love and to practice the purity of the visible church.[3]

In Christ's kingdom the lion and the lamb will lie down together peacefully. Such harmony needs to begin with us right now as we are conformed to God's image. The Lord can help us overcome the things that divide us. With his help we may take small but real steps toward healing. For this to happen, though, we must genuinely want to love and forgive those who have hurt us. Knowing how easily the best of intentions can go astray or be misconstrued, it is all the more necessary to be patient and persevere in our relationships rather than become discouraged when faced with less than a desired or expected response. Genuine friendships emerge from such perseverance. When the love of Christ guides our thoughts and actions, we discover a new capacity to love and honor others. When that happens, winsomeness and beauty characterize our relationships rather than mean-spiritedness, hatred, or arrogance.

Love Is the Glue

The key to relationships and true community, the real glue that holds us together, is love. Without it we are nothing, our efforts are nothing. No one has said it more eloquently than Paul. Speak with the tongues of angels, fathom all mysteries, possess all knowledge, have faith to move mountains, give everything you have to the poor, and give your body to the flames as a sacrifice, but no matter how much you do or how spectacular it may appear, without love you gain nothing (1 Cor. 13:1–3). Love never fails. Human effort without it does, reducing life to despair and ashes. Who wants to settle for that?

God is love (1 John 4:8, 16). Love permeates all that he is and everything that he does. Love provides the basis for his goodness, kindness, compassion, patience, and forgiveness. He delights to love. It also brings him joy when his grace takes root in our lives (Luke 15:10). Most of all it triggers his generosity. His greatest gift is that of his only begotten Son for our salvation (John 3:16; Rom. 5:8; 1 John 4:9–10). But he also provides everything else we need. As Paul argued, if he gave his own Son, isn't there every reason to believe he will provide anything else we need (Rom. 8:32)? God's hand is never closed to his children. Jesus asked, "Which of you, if his son asks for bread, will give him a stone? Or if he asks for a fish, will give him a snake?"

(Matt. 7:9–10). Then should you expect any less from your Father in heaven?

God's love is strong, and he can be tough when necessary. If, for your own good, chastening is required, he will do it (Heb. 12:6–11) rather than permissively stand on the periphery while you self-destruct. He sends trials to strengthen and he sends pain to correct. He will not smite you as he smote Jesus, but you may feel the sting of his corrective rod, perhaps more painfully if you stubbornly resist his will.

As God remakes you in his image, he will fill you with love for him and others. The reason you love him is because he loved you first; his gift of love in Christ changed everything (1 John 4:19). If you love him, you will also

> The closest human love encloses a potential germ of estrangement or hatred.
>
> **William James, *The Varieties of Religious Experience***

want to please him (John 15:9–10). This is done by obeying him and extending true love to others. When love is the driving force in a relationship, it changes the questions you ask and the decisions you make. In this light you understand why Jesus answered the Pharisees' question about the greatest commandment as he did: "Love the Lord your God with all your heart and with all your soul and with all your mind. This is the first and greatest commandment. And the second is like it: Love your neighbor as yourself" (Matt. 22:37–39).

Henri Nouwen, reflecting on this summary, warns us not to turn too quickly to our neighbor. He says we are tempted to do this while trying not to forget God, thus confusing our priorities. We must first love God—and love him completely—then we will find the capacity by his grace to love others too.[4]

We may have stressed the love of God for us so much that we have in turn failed to emphasize adequately the importance of loving God. Yet, love for God is foundational to our faith and our relationship with him. We must learn to love God profoundly as his beloved children. While there is no reason to display our love superficially or insensitively, that is no excuse to neglect the cultivation of our love for him. Knowing God means loving God.

The apostle John, attempting to help believers ascertain the authenticity of their faith, offered them three tests. One of those is love for each other. "We should love one another. . . . We know that we have passed from death to life, because we love our brothers. Anyone who does not love remains in death" (1 John 3:11, 14). Continuing his reasoning in the next chapter, he adds,

> Dear friends, let us love one another, for love comes from God. Everyone who loves has been born of God and knows God. Whoever does not love does not know God, because God is love. This is how God showed his love among us: He sent his one and only Son into the world that we might live through him. This is love: not that we loved God, but that he loved us and sent his Son as an atoning sacrifice for our sins. Dear friends, since God so loved us, we also ought to love one another. No one has ever seen God; but if we love one another, God lives in us and his love is made complete in us. . . . God is love. Whoever lives in love lives in God, and God in him.
>
> 1 John 4:7–12, 16

As John persistently pursues his point, he concludes by warning that love for God is inextricably connected to love for others. "If you cannot love the people who surround you daily," he argues, "then how can you love God?" The response is, "How can you say something like that? Of course I love God." "No," John replies. "If you

cannot love those who are near you and who have been
made in God's image, then how in the world can you love
the true and living God when you have never even seen
him?" (see 1 John 4:19–21). The more you think about it
the more cogent John's argument becomes as he works
from what you do see to what you don't see.

> Here, then, is a further corollary of the Trinitarian image.
> To be human, after the image and likeness of God the Holy
> Trinity, means to love others with a love that is costly and
> self-sacrificing. If God the Father so loved us that he gave
> his only-begotten Son to die for us on the Cross, if God the
> Son so loved us that he descended into hell on our behalf,
> then we shall only be truly in the image and likeness of
> the Trinity if we also lay down our lives for each other.
> Without *kenosis* and cross-bearing, without the exchange
> of substituted love and all the voluntary suffering which
> this involves, there can be no genuine likeness to the Trin-
> ity. "Let us love one another," we proclaim in the Liturgy,
> "that with one mind we may confess Father, Son and Holy
> Spirit, the Trinity consubstantial and undivided." With-
> out mutual love there is no true confession of faith in the
> Trinity. But "love one another" means "lay down your lives
> for one another."[5]

The Characteristics of Love

To take this a step further, as you are being remade in
the image of God through your spiritual pilgrimage, the
characteristics of his love will become more and more evident in your life. Patience, kindness, compassion, and forgiveness are the ways his love is expressed. Is it any surprise that the early influence of Christianity on American
values resulted in a demonstration of compassion and generosity? During the last century, a large proportion of
global charity emanated from America in response to nat-

ural disasters or suffering and deprivation resulting from political or military actions. Christian denominations set up medical missions and shipped huge amounts of needed supplies. That is what we should expect of real Christianity. As the spiritual maturation process takes place, more of these characteristics should find enduring expressions in your life. The possibilities are limitless.

True love also reaches out to the unlovely and seemingly unlovable, just as God reached out to us when we were his enemies (Rom. 5:10). Jesus pointed out that it is easy to love those who love you. The real test is to love those who give you every reason not to love them. That is not easy. The scribes of his day unhesitatingly insisted that you should hate your enemy just as surely as you should love your neighbor. Many people readily agreed, but Jesus said, "If you love those who love you, what credit is that to you? Even 'sinners' love those who love them. . . . But love your enemies, do good to them, and lend to them without expecting to get anything back" (Luke 6:32, 35).

Of course, other characteristics besides compassion and forgiveness are typical of genuine love. Paul provides a brief checklist in 1 Corinthians 13:4–7: "Love is patient, love is kind. It does not envy, it does not boast, it is not proud. It is not rude, it is not self-seeking, it is not easily angered, it keeps no record of wrongs. Love does not delight in evil but rejoices with the truth. It always protects, always trusts, always hopes, always perseveres."

To paraphrase his description, we could say that the kind of love God gives does not produce an inflated selfishness or an ego that is bent on gaining recognition, if necessary by bragging. Nor is love disturbed by the recognition or achievement of others. In addition, love is patiently forbearing and does not become upset or irritated by the faults or offenses of other people. There is no grudge bearing or record keeping regarding those problems. Love always seeks that which is appropriate and decent in a given situation even when it could demand its own way.

Love cannot rejoice in evil deeds, nor in the affliction and suffering that may fall upon bad people. Rather, love searches out things that are praiseworthy, rejoicing in the triumph of beauty, truth, and goodness. Love is filled with faith, even in the face of calamity. Love also gives birth to hope rather than pessimism. Love never gives up; it endures. When we experience human failings, as there always are, love such as this covers a multiple of errors. Self-effacing, accommodating people demonstrate far more spiritual maturity than the gifted individuals or celebrities who don't possess these qualities.

By contrast, when selfishness, mean-spiritedness, hardheartedness, and impatience are dominant character traits or are frequently expressed, their presence signals an absence of love or spiritual immaturity. Strange, isn't it, that someone who is gifted intellectually or is a scintillating speaker, yet cares for others only so far as he can use them for his own purposes, may be looked up to as a great Christian. Talent in tandem with a callused disregard for others, except as rungs on the ladder of recognition, may attract popular acclaim, but they are far from being a model of spiritual maturity. Our adulation of contemporary Christian celebrities is reminiscent of the Corinthian problem concerning giftedness. It is a sad commentary regarding the influence of secular standards on the church that such things occur, but they do. So celebrities, the rich, and the brilliant are adulated. Do not misunderstand me, it is not bad to be bright, rich, or famous, but as Paul noted, without the grace note of love, there is an annoying clang (cf. 1 Cor. 1:26–2:5; 13:1–2). Appreciate the gift but don't imitate the immaturity. This lesson must be learned and practiced or else Christianity will suffer tragic consequences.

Deceit and manipulation among Christian people is another reverse example. Rather than possessing the attributes of the servant, who is concerned for the greater good of others, many possess a perverse compulsion to get what they want through coercion or manipulation. Who knows how many people have been permanently scarred or completely repulsed by contact with such spiritually immature Christianity? How many churches or denominations bear the lasting scars of ego wars? Self-aggrandizing church politics has done more damage than we are able to assess.

Sometimes Christians fail to offer compassion when it is most needed, as in the case of Matthew Allen, who battled AIDS for all of his thirteen years as a result of a blood transfusion given to his mother during her pregnancy. When his father, Scott Allen, a pastor on the staff of a

> **The only place outside heaven where you can be perfectly safe from all the dangers and penetrations of love is hell.**
>
> C. S. Lewis, *The Four Loves*

church in Colorado, first became aware of this disastrous situation, he told his senior pastor, expecting to receive his concern and support. Instead, he was fired immediately. Matthew was removed from the church's day care center, and the family was told to find another church.

When the family moved to another state, church after church refused to enroll Matthew in Sunday school. They were afraid that by accepting an AIDS child, they would scare off members and prospective members of the church. Eventually, the family quit attending church altogether as a result of this experience. They expressed no desire to attend church again. When young Matthew was asked about it, he replied, "They kicked me out."

God cannot be pleased when he sees behavior such as this from church people who talk of faith and love. It is not the way of spirituality, much less spiritual maturity.

God's way brings healing, harmony, and beauty to human relationships. These are marks of spiritual maturity.[6]

Ultimately the measure of our conformity to God's love is not measured by how often we talk about it but by how it comes to expression in our lives, primarily through our relationships. When we love others, we put them first, not ourselves. We think of what is best for them. In spite of being hurt by them, we patiently persevere in these relationships and willingly forgive because we are not selfishly absorbed in what we receive. The welfare of others is our priority.

What really counts in life is not what you have but who you have. As the Bible says, a person's life does not consist of his or her abundance of possessions. If you want to measure God's love in your life, examine your relationships.

QUESTIONS FOR REFLECTION

1. What steps do you need to take to strengthen your relationship with God?
2. Think about the relationships you had with others when you became a Christian. What relational changes have occurred since then? Why?
3. What changes please you the most?
4. What relationships need mending or strengthening? What should you do about them?
5. What steps are you taking with those you find difficult to love?
6. What is the most important thing you learned from this chapter?

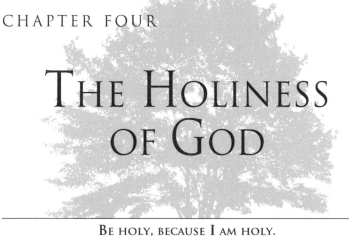

CHAPTER FOUR

THE HOLINESS OF GOD

BE HOLY, BECAUSE I AM HOLY.

LEVITICUS 11:44

D ietrich Rascher was training to become an SS officer in the German army. Before leaving home, he
had fallen in love with a lovely young girl named
Ernestine, but their budding romance was interrupted by
the demands of his new military life. As part of his rigor-
ous and thorough training, Rascher was to teach a puppy
to obey his every command. He and his dog stayed together
day and night, bonding closely in a short time. In fact,
Rascher developed such an attachment to her that he
named her Ernestine. They quickly became the superior
pair of all the cadets in training. Not only were they inseparable, they were perfectly meshed, as if one seamless unit.

69

Finally, the time arrived for Dietrich's graduation and the eagerly awaited receipt of the coveted SS dagger and black uniform. A few days before the ceremony, Dietrich and Ernestine were called into a stone room in the kennel. His Hauptsturm Führer was there and complimented him on his achievement.

"You have learned your lessons well. You will be a credit to the master race. Before receiving your SS dagger there is, however, a final obedience test that all SS men must take."

"Jawohl," Rascher snapped from his position to attention.

"You will, at this instant, choke your dog to death."

SS Kadett Dietrich Rascher passed his final test of obedience. With neither qualm, hesitation, nor visible show of personal emotion, he reached down, grabbed the trusting animal, put a choke hold on her and pressed quickly to snap her neck. He then came back to attention.

"With men like you," the captain congratulated, "we are undefeatable."[1]

This story, told by Leon Uris in *Armaggedon,* is a grim reminder of what can happen to the human race when moral absolutes are suspended. It has not always been this way. When God created Adam and Eve, they were sinless and upright. His prohibition, "You must not eat from the tree of the knowledge of good and evil" (Gen. 2:17), became for them not only a test of obedience but of commitment and loyalty.

Why they disobeyed is difficult to say, except that they failed miserably before the seductive temptation of the devil, who transformed the forbidden fruit into something irresistible. They disobeyed the Lord—knowingly they disobeyed—to their lasting shame. Their disobedience was inexcusable. Whatever excuse they mustered was vaporous because God's prohibition had been explicit. God's response to Cain might well have applied to them: "If you do what is right, will you not be accepted? But if you do not do what is right, sin is crouching at your door; it desires to have you, but you must master it" (Gen. 4:7).

However, now mastered by sin, for the first time in their existence they felt shame and hid from God, fruitlessly, of course. In spite of his warning, they had violated God's trust and love through their disobedience. Realizing too late what they had done (and that now they could not undo it), they tried to hide. But it is impossible to hide from God. He found them and, as a punishment for their disobedience, permanently expelled them from the Garden. That expulsion seemed severe, but the damage was far greater than that.

Paradise Lost

John Milton described the consequences of their sin as *Paradise Lost*. Stained with sin, corrupt within, and trying to cover their shame, they were a tragic pair. Not only had they spoiled their idyllic life in the Garden of Eden, they had contaminated and polluted human existence. Everyone born forever after—except Jesus—would be marked by that same sinful nature and would come under the judgment of God (Rom. 5:12, 14, 17–19). Once sin snaked its way into the human heart, anguish and evil followed. Trouble arrived sooner than anticipated, with catastrophic consequences. One of their young sons, Cain, murdered his brother Abel. By Noah's time, wickedness had proliferated so much that God was grieved in his heart at what he saw happening among the human race (Gen. 6:5–6). During Abraham's life, Sodom and Gomorrah so epitomized iniquity that God destroyed both cities and their inhabitants as a warning of his unwillingness to tolerate such evil. He made an example of them to restrain others from a similar embrace of iniquity.

The fall was the equivalent of opening Pandora's box. Once Adam and Eve sinned, all kinds of evil were loosed. Murder, sexual immorality, lying, stealing, drunkenness— the list goes on and on. Even King David, who was described as a man after God's own heart, was guilty of many of these evil deeds. The entire sweep of human history from biblical times onward has witnessed an incessant lust for money, sex, and power without regard to its acquisition or use. Because of sin, we lock our homes and our

> It is characteristic of those who are evil to judge others as evil. Unable to acknowledge their own imperfection, they must explain away their flaws by blaming others. And, if necessary, they will even destroy others in the name of righteousness.
>
> M. Scott Peck, *People of the Lie*

cars, install security systems, and protect important information. We watch ethnic cleansing and genocide on television. We see mutilated bodies, starving families, homeless children. A hacker silently and maliciously spreads a new virus across the Internet. A father kicks and beats his daughter, breaking bones and causing other internal injuries, then tells authorities she fell down the stairs. Teenagers on a rampage of rage and revenge gun down their classmates in a grisly slaughter at school. The price of the fall! Look at the policemen and troopers in your city, count the lawyers, note the security checks at the airport. The price of the fall!

Kenneth Cook, an Air Force weapons analyst with an outstanding record of achievement, was a highly regarded physicist and mathematician and was listed in American Men of Service. Asked to falsify reports, he refused. It so violated his conscience that he could not do it, even if commanded to do so. His integrity was too important to be sacrificed, regardless of the consequences. After all, he thought, if the government could not trust his reports, to what extent could it trust any other reports? So he complained that his commanding officer was distorting reports regarding the ICBM missile defense system.

Whistle blowers are unpopular, and Kenneth Cook was no exception. He was fired, declared incompetent, and denied due process of law. He could have sought another job without blowing the whistle, but he believed that truth would be rewarded and that he would be vindicated. He fought to be cleared and reinstated, but he was unsuccessful. He spent his money, including savings, on legal fees and court costs until all his resources were depleted. The hearings were kept private so no one knew what was happening to him. No one came to his rescue. He became another victim of a callused, bloated bureaucracy.

Reduced to living on a few hundred dollars a month from a pension, Cook walked miles just to save bus fare. His clothes became frayed and tattered. A meager diet took its toll, and he began to suffer from malnutrition. Impoverished and embittered, this man who simply wanted truth and justice finally dropped dead of a heart attack in a department store. Don't you wish this story could have a happy ending? Unfortunately, it didn't because this is the kind of world in which we find ourselves. Often people who try to do right suffer for it. Kenneth Cook is numbered among them.

Although the law of God is written on everyone's heart, as evidenced by conscience, people reject it so they can do what they want to do. They deny their accountability to God (Rom. 1:18–25; 2:14–15). They suppress the truth so they can believe what they want to believe and live the way they want to live. The strongest evidence of this in recent years is the rejection of moral absolutes. As Allan Bloom so aptly noted in *The Closing of the American Mind*, on every college campus students are convinced of one thing: Truth is relative.[2] Decisions are no longer seen as right and wrong but as choices or preferences. For example, abortion is not considered the wrongful taking of the life of an unborn child but rather the free choice of a pregnant woman who can decide whether to give birth to that child.

Recently, I received a letter from a perceptive young woman who had worshiped in an evangelical church the previous Sunday. She was surprised to hear the pastor say, "There are no biblical absolutes, only personal preferences." Even more surprising was the fact that three hundred parishioners were "nodding in mindless consent."

As one of the new spokesmen for such thinking, Richard Rorty said all we have is persuasion, politics, and power. Once the search for truth is abandoned as hopeless, then morality with its sense of right and wrong evaporates too. Choice becomes a matter of preference rather than morality. "I want" becomes the standard rather than "I should." People make choices and either do what they want to do or what someone else wants them to do. If life can be reduced to a quest for self-gratification, then people will more than likely attempt to persuade others to their way of thinking or use political means to achieve their desires. In some instances, a power play may be used when other efforts fail. Thus was born the phrase "hermeneutic of suspicion" as recognition that everyone has an agenda. People must discover what that hidden agenda is so that they know how they want to respond to it.

Righteousness and the Gospel

The gospel powerfully addresses the human condition spoiled by sin because Christ alone removes our sins and makes us acceptable to God. He was born for this reason. As Paul puts it, he was "born of a woman, born under the law, to redeem those under the law" (Gal. 4:4–5). He identified with us as a human through his incarnation, yet he was sinless. His birth by the Virgin Mary assured that in conception and birth—as well as the rest of his life—he would be sinless. He suffered and was tempted as we are, so that he sympathetically identifies with our struggles, yet he never yielded to sin (Heb. 4:14–15; 5:7–10). Though Adam succumbed to the charm of Satan's temptation, Christ steadfastly resisted, remaining perfectly obedient (Matt. 4:1–11).

His was no facile obedience—he struggled (Luke 22:39–46). Finally, he was crucified, dying the death of a curse, suffering the punishment that our sins deserve, to redeem us from the curse of the law (Gal. 3:10–14). For "God made him who had no sin to be sin for us, so that in him we might become the righteousness of God" (2 Cor. 5:21). As the sin of the first Adam brought judgment on the human race, the sinlessness and death of Christ brings hope. Those who trust in him receive the gift of righteousness and justification (Rom. 5:17–19).

Such a gift is necessary because we cannot remove our own sins. There is no way you or anyone can earn his or her own salvation because just one sin is enough to bring you under judgment, no matter how many good things you do (James 2:10). That is right—one sin. God's command is to be holy—without sin—which is humanly impossible because everyone has already sinned, violating God's command (Rom. 3:9–18, 23). Of course, everyone sins more than once, but regardless of the frequency, intensity, or severity, the consequences are judgment and eternal punishment (Rom. 6:23).

Luther's great discovery was that faith is the only avenue that leads to acceptance by God. Justification is and must be by faith and faith alone. When you turn from your sins in repentance and trust in Christ alone for the righteousness that you cannot achieve through your own effort, then you are accepted by God because of the sinless righteousness of Christ. You are justified by faith and declared pure and clean by God. Now you are acceptable to him.

Spiritual Growth and Morality

Once justified, the believer begins the process of being remade in the image of God. God is holy (Pss. 99:9; 111:9). His absolute moral purity and perfection add grandeur to his other attributes so that his power, wisdom, and love are completely pure. In his pure essence, God is a consuming fire (Deut. 24:4). The majestic glory of his holiness is such that no one can look directly at him and live. His pure essence must be muted in some way—as by the pillar of fire or cloud. Even then, his holiness emits such transcendent majesty that mere mortals tremble in his presence. No wonder Jacob exclaimed with astonishment after he had wrestled with the angel all night, "I saw God face to face, and yet my life was spared" (Gen. 32:30). Yet he had not seen God as he really is, rather he saw what is called a theophany, or revelation of God—in this instance in human form.

When Moses left Mount Sinai, his face glowed with a radiance that was unnatural because he had been in God's presence (Exod. 34:29–32). For Isaiah, it was enough to have a vision of the Lord high and lifted up surrounded by the cherubim who, covering their faces, shouted "Holy, holy, holy." That vision of the majestic holiness of God traumatized Isaiah, who exclaimed, "'Woe to me!' . . . 'I am ruined! For I am a man of unclean lips'" (Isa. 6:5). The Bible frequently reminds us that God is incomparably great and holy: "Who is like you—majestic in holiness, awesome in glory, working wonders?" (Exod. 15:11).

The word *holy* does not appear in the biblical narrative until Exodus 3:5, when God speaks to Moses at the burning bush. From that point, it was used in regard to the covenant and the law so that there is a link between holiness and righteousness. Because God is holy, he is also just. He cannot permissively look on evil and pass it by. He is compelled by his nature to deal justly with it at some point, whether sooner or later. Consider, for example, the way his holiness and justice are linked to the deaths of Nadab and Abihu (Lev. 10:1–3; cf. Num. 16:35). The Bible says they offered a profane or unauthorized fire before the Lord, which suggests that they did not follow instructions

> **Nowhere is the singular uniqueness of the God of the Bible more evident than in the Christian vision of the good and the right that Scripture commands and nurtures.**
>
> Carl F. H. Henry, *Christian Countermoves in a Decadent Culture*

for offering incense. Their disobedient worship resulted in judgment rather than forgiveness. It is reminiscent of the judgment that fell on Cain because of his disobedient worship. The commentary on the judgment of Nadab and Abihu is: "Among those who approach me I will show myself holy" (Lev. 10:3).

Because God is holy, we seek holiness as a sign of our identity with him, and as we do, holiness becomes a mark of our spiritual growth. We often refer to holiness as morality. We accept God's standards of right and wrong, committing ourselves to them. We reject the immorality of unbelievers because we are, as Paul put it, "created to be like God in true righteousness and holiness" (Eph. 4:24). Obedience is the key. Adam and Eve disobeyed; Jesus was perfectly obedient. Now our obedience, by faith, will mark our conformity to God's standards of morality.

Obedience

You now have a new motivation because of what God has done for you through Christ. You love him, you want to show your gratitude, you want to please him. As you look for the best way to please him, you discover that he has told you how to do it: obey him. Do what he says.

As John persistently points out, this is a good test of the genuineness of your faith. "This is love for God: to obey his commands. And his commands are not burdensome" (1 John 5:3). The hymn has it right: "For there is no other way to be happy in Jesus, but to trust and obey." You cannot, however, do it by your own strength; God's grace through the Holy Spirit is essential. With the Spirit's help, you will want to obey, and the more you grow spiritually, the more your commitment to obedience will be strengthened.

Scripture emphatically states that obedience is more important to God than worship (1 Sam. 15:22; Isa. 1:10–20). This may be contrary to popular practice, but this is exactly what Jesus and the apostles taught. The Sermon on the Mount, referred to earlier, describes how a child of God should live. To that end, Jesus clarified God's expectations over against what some people, including the Pharisees, said. He declared that claiming to belong to God, through participation in religious activities and deeds, does not make you belong. Rather, doing the will of the Father in heaven identifies a believer (Matt. 7:21). His concluding illustration drove home this point. The wise man puts these words into practice (7:24), while the foolish man who also hears these words does not practice them (7:26).

Obedience, born of faith and love, builds character and develops integrity. It takes "the form of a single-minded passion to please by love and loyalty, devotion and praise."[3] As believers put off the old self, with its former way of living, and put on the new, "created to be like God in true righteousness and holiness," they become more and more unlike the secular, pagan world. They become children of light in a world of darkness (Eph. 4:22–24; 5:8–11). Paul contrasts these two ways of life with specific words that describe the difference: truth versus falsehood, stealing versus working and sharing, malice versus forgiveness, and so on (Eph. 4:7–5:20).

Historically, holiness has been a leading mark of evangelical people, just as it has been a central emphasis among their teachers. Think of Luther's stress on faith producing good works and of Calvin's insistence on the third use of the law as code and spur for God's children. Think of the Puritans demanding a changed life as evidence of regeneration and hammering away at the need for everything in personal and community life to be holiness to the Lord. Think of the Dutch and German Pietists stressing the need for a pure heart expressed in a pure life and of John Wesley proclaiming that "scriptural holiness" was Methodism's main message. Think of the so-called holiness revival of the second half of the nineteenth century and of the classic volume by J. C. Ryle, *Holiness* (still in print and selling well after 100 years), and of the trust of the thought of such latter-day teachers as Oswald Chambers, Andrew Murray, A. W. Tozer, Watchman Nee, and John White. In the past, the uncompromising evangelical quest for holiness was awesome in its intensity. Yet that which was formerly a priority and a passion has become a secondary matter for us who bear the evangelical name today.[4]

How should the holiness of God come to expression in your life as you become more and more like the Lord through your love for him and your obedience to him? What will help you to be less like the world and demonstrate that you are now set apart for God? The words that most quickly come to mind are *purity, righteousness, justice, faithfulness, truthfulness,* and *integrity.* This list, though incomplete and merely suggestive, contains specific traits that reveal whether our morality measures up to God's expectations.

Purity and Righteousness

Purity and *righteousness* are high-sounding but empty terms unless we have a standard of measurement, in this instance, the will of God as revealed in Scripture. God has clearly commanded that those who follow him must not steal, murder, commit adultery, give false testimony, or covet (Exod. 20:1–17). Wherever he reveals his will to us in the Bible, in the Ten Commandments, or elsewhere, we are obligated to obey as his followers. To ignore or repudiate his directions displeases him and estranges us, unless we genuinely repent of our disobedience and redirect our efforts.

Righteousness reflects an alignment of action with God's law. Just as God's law is a true expression of his nature, as one who is far above us in his righteousness and purity, so his actions are in accord with his law. God always does what is right because it is his nature to do so. He cannot do otherwise or he would not be true to himself (Gen. 18:25). We may also properly conclude that he commands only what is right for the same reason.

The Christian who is being conformed to the righteousness of God, therefore, must try to bring his or her life into conformity with God's law as revealed in the Bible. That alignment includes one's thoughts and feelings as

> Whenever you find a man who says he does not believe in a real Right and Wrong, you will find the same man going back on this a moment later. He may break his promise to you, but if you try breaking one to him, he will be complaining, "It's not fair."
>
> C. S. Lewis, *Mere Christianity*

well as actions. Christians who love God also love his law. His commandments are no longer burdensome but a source of joy and satisfaction (1 John 5:2–3). If you love God, then nothing makes you happier than doing what delights him. If you really want to obey God and keep his commandments, you must go beyond superficial compliance to a genuine understanding of the intent of each commandment. Once you understand that intent, you may begin to bring your life into alignment with it. The Pharisees' problem was that while they appeared to be enthusiastic and sincere about obeying the law, they used the words to construct their own code of conduct, a code that often missed the true intent of God's law. Rather than being the most zealous keepers and perpetuators of the law, they were actually leading people to misunderstand and disobey it. In their own perverse way, they were on a course to destroy the law.

That is why in the Sermon on the Mount Jesus went to great pains to point out that although it had been said a person should not commit adultery, the real intent of the law was to assure sexual purity and to underscore the sanctity of marriage. So if you have a sinful lust, a sexual titillation when you look at another person, then you have sinned. Moreover, if you marry someone, you are joined to that person through the physical bond of sex, as well as your love, which creates a deep bond of trust and belonging, making possible through this unique relationship a sublime experience that is like a taste of heaven. Once married, if you become sexually involved with another person or divorce your spouse without a God-given reason, you are guilty of adultery and may cause the other party to become guilty (Matt. 5:27–32; 1 Cor. 6:13–7:9). Not only that, you jeopardize, if not destroy, that uniquely beautiful relationship the Lord has given to you and your spouse. Would you relinquish a taste of heaven for a few minutes of physical passion?

Principles underlie each of the Lord's commandments, and we must attempt to understand them as well as their implications if we intend to conform to God's expectations. Therefore, it is important to ask why the command "you shall not steal" was given. What is implied by this commandment? How did God intend for it to shape our lives? It is readily apparent that there are principles underlying this commandment such as the right to possess property, the right to work and to earn so that you can purchase and possess. Because you have the right of ownership or possession, you may not take or steal what belongs to someone else. Paul seems to have taken this a step further by insisting that once you become a believer, not only are you prohibited from stealing but you have a responsibility to work so that you will have enough to share with those who are needy in addition to providing for your own needs (Eph. 4:28). The mature believer will not steal, nor will he selfishly cling to what he has, but will gladly share of his abundance with the poor. We gradually grasp the fact that the right to work and possess creates an opportunity for good stewardship, which in its turn makes possible generosity to others. How different from the selfish accumulation of one whom Jesus referred to as a rich fool.

In regard to the command "do not kill," a person may say, "I have never murdered anyone so I have not broken the commandment." Of course, murder is wrong, but Jesus showed that the intent of the commandment goes beyond a prohibition against murder. He taught that the emotions that could eventually lead to murder are also wrong and forbidden. That is why Jesus said you must not be angry with your brother. Anger, in this instance, should be distinguished from indignation regarding evil, for it is different. That is why Paul can say, "In your anger do not sin," adding, "get rid of all bitterness, rage and anger" (Eph. 4:26, 31). The point Jesus made is that you must not harbor resentment or ill feelings toward another person. Anger will eat away at you and can eventually destroy you as well as others. You need to be at peace with everyone. If you are not, talk to those whom you are angry with and work out the problems.

The point here is clear enough: If you love others, you will not want to hurt them or take what they have. If anything, you will want to help them and give them comfort.

Greed, resentment, hostility, hatred, and callused disregard for the welfare of others are signs of a flawed spirituality. God expects more from those who love him. As a
matter of fact, Jesus pushed the point by saying that you
must not love only your brother, you must also love the
enemy who hates you and tries to destroy you. There is
no special virtue in loving only those who love you. Anyone can do that. God sends the rain to the unjust as well
as the just, so if we would be like him, we must treat our
enemies as Jesus wants us to treat them (Matt. 5:43–48).

As you review the Sermon on the Mount, you cannot
dismiss the compelling moral claims placed upon the
Christian, a morality deeply rooted in the enduring moral
law of the Old Testament (Matt. 5:17–20). This morality
must not be taken lightly or superficially because it is
supremely important to God and critical to our identity
as those who have the attributes of our Father in heaven.
The care Jesus gave to correct misinterpretation and misunderstanding of moral obligation reveals the far-reaching implications of God's moral law.

When God redeems his people, he cleanses and purifies
them from their sinful deeds that have contaminated them
and made them dirty. Such sinfulness is repugnant to him;
he will not tolerate it. Malachi refers to the effect of the
awesome appearance of God as "a refiner's fire or a laun-
derer's soap. He will sit as a refiner and purifier of silver. . . .
Then the LORD will have men who will bring offerings in
righteousness" (Mal. 3:2–3). The purity laws and rituals of
purification in the Old Testament underscore God's necessary work of cleansing his people so that they will be
acceptable to him, the holy God. That is undoubtedly why
the New Testament picks up on this imagery of purification in salvation as being washed and cleansed (1 Cor. 6:11;
Heb. 9:13–14). Christians are obligated "to purify ourselves
from everything that contaminates body and spirit, perfecting holiness out of reverence for God" (2 Cor. 7:1).

In calling us to purity, God calls us to eliminate sin from our lives. That is why John says, "Everyone who has this hope in him purifies himself, just as he is pure" (1 John 3:3). Although again and again we will not be able to keep ourselves from sinning, we must try. With every fiber of our being, we must attempt to stamp out evil thoughts and deeds. This can be frustrating because sin is so doggedly persistent. Nevertheless, we must strive to rise above the sins that formerly enslaved us. We must put them to death (Rom. 8:12–13). Then, of course, through the grace of the Lord, as we confess our sins, we have his promise that he will "forgive us our sins and purify us from all unrighteousness" (1 John 1:9).

At least two errors may develop when you begin to apply God's moral law: legalism and hypocrisy. Hypocrisy includes paying lip service to Christianity with pious statements or superficial adherence while ignoring the responsibilities and moral obligations of the faith. Such an attitude has helped to create conditions in which no significant difference in moral ethical behavior between church members and non-church members can be found. This has done much to discredit Christianity. If there is no significant difference between the way Christians and non-Christians think and live, why should anyone bother to become a Christian?

One example of hypocrisy comes from the early church and is recorded in Acts 4:32–5:11. In this instance, Ananias and Sapphira acted as if they had sold a piece of property and given all the proceeds to the church just as other believers had done, when, in fact, they had kept some of the money. Though they had every right to do so, they tried to deceive their fellow Christians into thinking they had given everything they had received. Pretenders! Some of Jesus' most searing words were directed toward hypocrisy (Matthew 23). He compared hypocrites to whitewashed tombs, which are "beautiful on the outside, but on the inside are full of dead men's bones and everything unclean" (Matt. 23:27–28).

One day during a conversation, a friend confessed his cynicism to me regarding businessmen who referred to themselves as Christians just so they could attract business. He said, according to his experience, such a practice typically camouflaged incompetence or deceit. Seldom did he have a good business experience with someone who used Christianity as a point of contact to do business. Whenever he encountered such an attitude, it was like a red flag. "Stop, be very careful before you proceed." Such was his experience with hypocrisy.

Legalism consists of reducing an important principle to a list of rules. A legalistic person might give the appearance of keeping the law but usually misses the true intent. To correct this kind of misunderstanding was undoubtedly a concern of Jesus when he preached the Sermon on

> And as the Scripture plainly teaches that practice is the best evidence of the sincerity of professing Christians; so reason teaches the same thing. Reason shows that men's deeds are better and more faithful interpretations of their minds than their words.
>
> Jonathan Edwards, *Religious Affections*

the Mount. One encounter between the Pharisees and Jesus regarding his activities on the Sabbath well illustrates the problems posed by legalism. The Pharisees, consummate legalists, had devised a complicated set of restrictions regarding Sabbath observance, stipulating in great detail what could and could not be done on that day. They had a list of thirty-nine categories of work, each of which was subdivided into six categories. These restrictions were burdensome, but Jesus did not allow their rules to restrict him because he understood the true intent of God's law (Mark

2:23–3:6). As Paul later observed to the Corinthians, "The letter kills, but the Spirit gives life" (2 Cor. 3:6).

Legalism has also created some lasting problems, especially for evangelicals. In some circles, emphasis was placed on social practices such as smoking, drinking, dancing, movies, television, and certain kinds of music. Consider the matter of drinking alcoholic beverages. The emergence of the Temperance Movement in the nineteenth century was intended to correct the problems of drunkenness, alcoholism, and their attendant excesses. It gradually hardened into abstinence, finally total abstinence—with a capital "T" for "Teetotaler." This eventually led to Prohibition and an amendment to the Bill of Rights in 1919. As a result of this crusade, in many Christian communities it became sinful to drink any alcoholic beverage. It was considered incompatible with genuine Christianity. Yet this position, though strenuously advocated by a substantial number of evangelicals, fails to find clear biblical support.

In the first place, the Bible does not condemn the consumption of alcohol, though it does condemn drunkenness with absolute clarity (Rom. 13:13; Gal. 5:19–21; Eph. 5:18; 1 Peter 4:2–3). As one whose father was an alcoholic and who was an unwilling and painful witness to the destructiveness of alcoholism, it was difficult for me to conclude that any form of alcoholic consumption was anything other than an unmitigated evil. I was eventually forced by Scripture to change my mind. The first miracle Jesus performed at Cana, turning the water into wine, and not only wine but the best wine that was offered at the wedding, is difficult to reconcile with enforced abstinence (John 2:1–11). To abstain as a matter of prudence or for conscience' sake is one thing; to legislate that Christians may never drink alcoholic beverages without committing a sin is another matter. Such an attitude is legalistic because there is no biblical basis for such a prohibition. The evidence in the Old and New Testaments is to the contrary (Gen. 27:28; Isa. 55:1;

1 Tim. 5:23). Although it may be wise not to consume alcoholic beverages, you cannot flatly declare it to be sinful or a condition of Christian obedience.

Paul bluntly addressed legalistic practices such as these:

> Since you died with Christ to the basic principles of this world, why, as though you still belonged to it, do you submit to its rules: "Do not handle! Do not taste! Do not touch!"? These are all destined to perish with use, because they are based on human commands and teachings. Such regulations indeed have an appearance of wisdom, with their self-imposed worship, their false humility and their harsh treatment of the body, but they lack any value in restraining sensual indulgence.
>
> Colossians 2:20–23

In spite of such biblical warnings, new problems or greater social tensions often provide fresh motivation to solve them by writing a new set of rules for Christian behavior, going beyond what the Bible legislates. The intent is usually noble, but if you add to what the Bible requires and demand that others comply with your new rules, you are guilty of legalism.

After encountering the unsettling demands of legalism and experiencing its bitter fruit, you may be inclined to ask, "Why emphasize obedience to the law of God? Isn't that a form of legalism too?" If obedience were promoted as a way to earn your salvation by doing enough good deeds, that might be true. But no one can do enough good deeds or be sufficiently obedient because God calls everyone to be holy as he is holy (Lev. 20:7; 1 Peter 1:15). One single disobedient act ruins all our good because a failure to be completely holy puts us under his judgment. The only solution is the gospel. When we become believers and want to please God, however, his expressed will for us by commandments and other precepts becomes our guide. We know that we cannot continue to live as we did before our conversion. We must try to change. Paul puts it this way: "Shall we go on sinning so that grace may increase? By no means! We died to sin; how can we live in it any longer?" (Rom. 6:1). Therefore, through the enabling grace of the Holy Spirit, we obey his commands and to the greatest degree possible conform to his will.

Justice

Leaving our discussion of the righteousness of God and its implications for our sanctification, let us consider how we may mirror the justice of God, which is also a mark of morality. Just as God shows no favoritism but is impartial and just in his dealings, so justice demands the same of a believer (Deut. 32:4; Rom. 2:6–11). A balanced understanding and application of God's Word should result in fair treatment, which means you expect to get what you deserve and you treat other people fairly. Spiritual maturity leads you to pay a fair amount for work or services rendered rather than as little as possible. In turn, you expect a fair return in effort and skill. This does not, of course, rule out grace or mercy, but it does underscore the necessity to be fair and just in all dealings.

The character of God is also mirrored in indignation due to injustice, such as exploitation of the weak. For example, paying extremely low wages to children who are forced to work for ten to fourteen hours a day in hot, crowded rooms with dangerous machines should raise the ire of discerning Christians, as should the dislocation and slaughter of citizens by a malignant government. When someone commits an atrocious crime and then is acquitted on a technicality, the public groans. Christians especially should be concerned that justice is served both as a deterrent to other potential evildoers and as a reminder that evil should be punished because of the damage it has caused. Whenever possible, restoration should follow. The path to spiritual maturity leads to a concern for justice so that God's moral code may come to full expression, bringing benefits and blessing to the entire community of believers and unbelievers.

Understandably, not every injustice can be addressed. As any parent knows, you cannot deal with every problem and every mistake. But the most important matters must be dealt with, and as they are, lesser wrongs will also decrease. If relatively insignificant matters are substantially addressed while more important matters are ignored, injustice occurs. Unfortunately, it is this uneven application that often creates frustration. We need to be selective and set priorities. Christians often have a greater influence on the selection process than we realize. As we mature spiritually, our biblical understanding and discernment should increase accordingly, bringing us the strength to be different when truth and justice require it.

As moral standards have unraveled in the United States and the last forty years have witnessed a more rapid declension than any comparable period in American history, there has been a rising level of restlessness and concern. No one really wants to live in a world of violence, sexual infidelity, and theft, especially if they become the victims. On the other hand, there is often an unwillingness to come to grips with the issues by punishing wrongdoers and requiring conformity to moral standards. Yet it is difficult to have one without the other. The mature believer knows the wages of sin are death because God is just. The soul that sins will surely die (Ezek. 18:4). Likewise, crime must not be allowed to pay. Moral standards will not long prevail without a commitment to justice.

Faithfulness

Another characteristic of morality is faithfulness. The Lord keeps his promises, and his mercies never fail. In

Lamentations we find the acknowledgement, "Great is your faithfulness" (3:23). Just as God is steadfast and faithful because of his inner character, so believers should reflect a similar resolve and constancy as they become spiritually mature (Exod. 34:6–7; James 1:17). Our commitment to the Lord must be permanent because he does not tolerate a fickle spirit. Unfaithfulness is repulsive to him, like adultery in marriage. The mature believer who imitates God

> But anyone who tries to recover the knowledge of sins these days must overcome long odds. To put it mildly, modern consciousness does not encourage moral reproach; in particular it does not encourage self-reproach.
>
> **Cornelius Plantinga, *Not the Way It's Supposed to Be***

strives to be trustworthy and loyal. Commitment to the Lord must be confirmed and unshakable, leading to "a long obedience in the same direction," as Eugene Peterson puts it. Marriage is a helpful analogy because it is often used in the Bible to describe God's relationship to his people. Marriage thrives on trust and crumbles without it. Trust cannot be established without the kind of commitment that brings reliable, consistent, unshakable behavior. You must know what you can depend on in order to trust.

Loyalty is directly related to faithfulness. It would hardly qualify in a contemporary list of virtues, largely because of the way self-interest dominates most decisions and relationships. If you get a better deal, you take it. Don't worry about leaving others in the lurch. Cutting costs? Slash a few staff, even if they have invested years with the company. Don't hesitate to leave a company that has invested thousands of dollars in your training if you can get a better deal and take privileged information with you. What happens if you trash your friends because you become bored with them or no longer need them? If you use people with no regard for their feelings or well-being, how can you justify that? Christians value commitment, honoring it with the gift of loyalty. When loyalty is given, then it is the responsibility of a believer to recognize and reward it. We often fail to do so, yet we complain about the loss of community and lack of relationships.

Faithfulness also means reliability and dependability. When God commits to do something, he follows through (Ps. 132:11; Heb. 6:17–18). He keeps his promises. To keep his covenant promise of redemption, God ultimately had to take the punishment for covenant breaking upon himself. That is why Jesus came into the world—to die for us. We should imitate Christ if our desire is to be like him. It is vital for us to keep our word. Once we have agreed to do something, we must do it regardless of the inconvenience or sacrifice involved (Ps. 15:4). If we agree to do a job at a certain time, we should do it. If we promise to be present at a meeting, we should be there. If we promise to do something but fail to deliver, what should the other party expect the next time, and what will he or she think of Christianity?

Faithfulness also contains elements of constancy and consistency. These characteristics don't preclude changing your mind when there is good reason to do so. Nor do they imply that creativity and innovation are always bad. Rather, they mean that the Christian who is being conformed to God's image is out of character if he changes every time the wind blows in a different direction (Eph. 4:14). Christians should be thought of as anchors rather than weather vanes. Stability, dependability, and reliability are essential to faithfulness, which in turn is essential to morality, which reflects the character of God.

Truthfulness

God reveals the truth, speaks the truth, and is the truth (Isa. 45:19; John 14:6). He is the true and living God (Jer. 10:10; John 17:3), and he cannot lie because he is the truth (Heb. 6:18). Those who are being conformed to his image learn to love the truth and stand for the truth. They are advocates of honesty and its best exemplars. Mason Weems made George Washington a paragon of virtue for his honesty in admitting he cut down a cherry tree. Ironically, the account is fictitious. But Christians above all people should be known for honesty and truthfulness. That is why Paul, referring to our calling to be like God in true righteousness and holiness, says, "Therefore each of you must put off falsehood and speak truthfully to his neighbor" (Eph. 4:25). The Bible also calls us to speak truthfully of others (Exod. 20:16).

On the other hand, deceitfulness and duplicity do not fit the pattern of biblical morality that finds its origin in the character of God. That is why one of the commandments is directed toward bearing false witness against others. When you cannot take another person at his word, you cannot trust that person. In this respect, truthfulness is a cornerstone of Christian morality.

Integrity

The more you learn about God, the more you recognize that he is completely consistent in every possible way. Who he is and what he does are vitally connected so that his actions flow directly and naturally from his person. There is no confusion or contradiction in him. This is what we would expect of God, and it is a reflection of his absolute integrity. We, on the other hand, are marked by inconsistencies. The clearer our understanding becomes of what God wants us to be, however, the more consistent we will be in translating that understanding into appropriate behavior. Spiritual growth in this sense is especially challenging for it requires the development of understanding. It also demands the ability to integrate disparate elements into a unified whole. The more we achieve alignment between our commitments or values and our behavior, the more we will reflect integrity.

Unfortunately, integrity is a missing dimension in much of contemporary society and is often a glaring deficiency in our leaders. Recently some lists of desired traits in business leaders ranked integrity, or character, at the top of the list, both underscoring its absence by calling attention to it as the highest priority and registering a keen desire for it. Should God expect less of believers who are supposed to reflect his character to an unbelieving world?

The Fruit of Morality

When these characteristics find expression in our lives, a number of benefits accrue. First, faithfulness creates a positive climate of trust and a stable environment in which people know what to expect. Such an environment reduces stress and frees people to concentrate on constructive, creative tasks. When people don't know what to expect and must live or work in a rapidly changing environment, they are more cautious and guarded.

Second, firm adherence to a clear moral standard provides the best basis on which to resist evil. Unless you are clearly persuaded of what is right, it is difficult to determine what is wrong, much less oppose it. All you have to do is review history to identify those who have been willing to resist evil regardless of the cost. If you cannot be certain of what is right, you will be less inclined to give it your enthusiastic, unreserved support, much less sacrifice for it.

Third, commitment to clear standards of morality motivates us to strive for the best rather than settle for mediocrity. As a young boy I was taught,

> Good, better, best,
> Never let it rest
> Till the good is better
> And the better is best.

Paul stated it memorably in Philippians 4:8: "Finally, brothers, whatever is true, whatever is noble, whatever is right, whatever is pure, whatever is lovely, whatever is admirable—if anything is excellent or praiseworthy, think about such things."

Fourth, this commitment to God's standard of morality makes us keenly aware of our dependence on him for constant help and continuing forgiveness. When we learn to love what is right and true, we also learn how impossible it is always to act on what we know and love. As we progress, we actually become more aware of our failings and our need for the Savior. The more we learn and the more we eliminate certain sins from our lives, the more aware we become of our remaining ignorance and of our lingering sinfulness. Take Paul as an example. From the righteous status he perceived himself to have prior to his conversion, he steadily descended after he came to faith in Christ (Phil. 3:4–6). He spoke of being the least of the apostles early in his ministry. Later he referred to himself as the least of all God's people. Toward the end of his ministry, he referred to himself as the worst of sinners (1 Cor. 15:9; Eph. 3:8; 1 Tim. 1:15). Notice how the more he grew spiritually, the more aware he became of his sinfulness and need for forgiveness. So it should be with each believer. Rather than developing arrogant self-righteous attitudes, we should be humbled and become more dependent on the Lord than ever, making the prayer of Robert Murray

McCheyne our own: "Lord, make me as holy as it is possible for a saved sinner to be."[5]

QUESTIONS FOR REFLECTION

1. What is the relationship of God's holiness to our morality?
2. List as many words as you can that reflect the holiness of God.
3. Why didn't Christians have a more favorable influence on culture during the twentieth century?
4. How are you different morally from non-Christians?
5. What is the most important thing you learned from this chapter?

CHAPTER FIVE

THE ONLY WISE GOD

MY PURPOSE IS THAT THEY MAY BE ENCOURAGED IN HEART AND UNITED IN LOVE, SO THAT THEY MAY HAVE THE FULL RICHES OF COMPLETE UNDERSTANDING, IN ORDER THAT THEY MAY KNOW THE MYSTERY OF GOD, NAMELY, CHRIST, IN WHOM ARE HIDDEN ALL THE TREASURES OF WISDOM AND KNOWLEDGE.

COLOSSIANS 2:2–3

God knows everything (1 John 3:20). Nothing can be hidden from him. Nothing is too difficult or complex for him to understand. His knowledge of the universe is limitless and inexhaustible because he is the creator (Psalm 139; Heb. 4:13). We cannot begin to know what God knows, for our knowledge of him is imperfect. When we search the Scriptures, however, we begin to catch a glimpse of the immensity and profundity of his knowledge. As Paul eloquently wrote,

Oh, the depth of the riches of the wisdom and knowledge
    of God!
  How unsearchable his judgments,
    and his paths beyond tracing out!
Who has known the mind of the Lord?
    Or who has been his counselor?
Who has ever given to God,
    that God should repay him?
For from him and through him and to him are all
    things.
  To him be the glory forever! Amen.

Romans 11:33–36

In an earlier age this kind of knowledge doubtlessly would have been awe inspiring, but in our information age it seems absolutely overwhelming. Now that we have begun to grasp the vastness of the cosmos, fight our way through the incessant stream of data inundating us daily, and struggle to master the intricate complexities of life, we realize how impossible it is for anyone to gather all the facts and understand them. It is almost impossible for experts to keep up with developments in their own fields of specialization, much less know everything.

But God knows absolutely everything—and he can put it all together so that it fits! This is one lesson to be gleaned from the Book of Job, for as the Lord speaks to Job about his circumstances and his inability to understand why traumatic things have happened to him, God reminds Job of the vastness and complexity of the world (Job 38–41). Much of it Job neither understands nor controls. God asks, "Where were you when I laid the earth's foundation? Tell me, if you understand. . . . What is the way to the abode of light? And where does the darkness reside? . . . Who has the wisdom to count the clouds?" (Job 38:4, 19, 37). "What good is a hippopotamus or a crocodile?" (see Job 40:15–41:34). He might have added, "Why do we have

97

rats, fleas, and diseases?" By way of this dialogical confrontation, the Lord reminds Job that he made the universe and he still controls it. Therefore, he knows why everything exists and why things happen as they do. Such knowledge was beyond human understanding and too wonderful for Job and the psalmist to comprehend (Job 42:3; Ps. 139:6).

The Fall and Human Understanding

Adam and Eve possessed a knowledge of God and creation that was enviable. Adam innately knew, for example, the name that was most appropriate for each animal (Gen. 2:19–20). They obviously knew a great deal more too, but Moses, in his account, makes no effort to specify the extent of their knowledge. Still, we have enough information in this brief record to be suitably impressed. On the other hand, Adam and Eve did not know everything. The tree of the knowledge of good and evil symbolized what they did not know, and God withheld it from them as a test. Satan saw their vulnerability regarding the tree and directed his attack at their weakness. The great temptation was an offer of knowledge, a knowledge that would enable Adam and Eve to be like God. Accepting the appealing half-truths of the serpent deprived them of the knowledge and experience they could have had by obeying God. The knowledge they subsequently gained by eating the forbidden fruit was not at all what they had expected. What they now knew, but might have avoided through obedience, was the painful, difficult side of life, and this knowledge led to sweat and toil, weeds and thistles, manipulation and murder. They now knew fear. They knew shame. They eventually would know suffering and death. They knew what it means to live under the wrath and judgment of

God. They knew they would have been better off without this knowledge.

As a result of the fall, they also had a faulty knowledge of themselves and their world. Their descendants would not even be aware of the extent of this deficiency, that is, that their knowledge was faulty. Job certainly is representative of this faulty knowledge, though his heart was right. Solomon is showcased as an example of a wise king, yet his understanding was deficient as well. As a result, God sent prophets to explain what he was doing in human history and why he was doing it. He explained the origin of the world and his relationship to the human race. In doing so, God made clear the response of repentance and faith that he expected from them. He gave this information, much of it now recorded as the Old Testament, so that people could understand his plan to redeem them.

The problem is that unbelievers have a hard time understanding and accepting God's message. They twist and distort it in various ways so that it becomes something entirely different from the message he originally delivered to them. God places an awareness of his existence in every person— a residual knowledge that results from being made in his image. But as Paul observed, "They exchanged the truth of God for a lie" (Rom. 1:25). Claiming to be wise, they became fools. They rejected the truth about God and the gospel as nonsense. But it was not the gospel that was foolish; they were foolish (Rom. 1:21–22; 1 Cor. 2:14). Sin adversely affects our understanding, causing us to distort the information we receive, especially spiritual truth. Because of sin, we can never assume that a person accurately hears and understands what has been said or accurately sees and comprehends what has occurred. This is a fundamental reason for miscommunication and misunderstanding.

One afternoon while I was visiting in a home, the clock struck the hour—its chime a series of beautiful, mellow notes. After a few moments, when the conversation permitted, I commented favorably about the clock. "Thank you," replied the owner. "It is interesting you should mention it. That clock was an anniversary present, and when we received it about a year ago, I heard it chime every hour. It even woke me up at night for the first few days. Now I never notice it, and if you had not said something, I would not have paid any attention to it." She had learned to filter that sound from her consciousness so that she no

> **The scandal of the evangelical mind is that there is not much of an evangelical mind.**
>
> Mark Noll, *The Scandal of the Evangelical Mind*

longer heard the chimes. We respond to stimuli in the same way, noticing or not noticing, perceiving or not perceiving. As long as our response does not create a problem or seems to function well, we continue the pattern. This is the way we normally operate because we cannot afford to give equal attention to every stimulus. We selectively note what seems to us to have significance.

Unfortunately, with the flow of years, especially the last two hundred years, there has been a gradually increasing tendency, now a prevailing pattern, to exclude God from what people think and do. In recent years there has been a persistent effort to remove God from the public square and to deny that he has any real practical influence on daily life so that apart from church-related matters and one's private faith, God is irrelevant. According to Craig Gay, this development has been abetted by a practical atheism that has gradually become deeply embedded in the cultural institutional realities of modern society.[1] Most people are completely unaware of this trend, focusing instead on current social or political issues. The current state of affairs may actually be far worse than people realize, according to Gay, who warns that "perhaps at no other time in history has the structural coherence of a social order depended less upon religious and/or theological understanding than it does today in modern societies."[2]

This is not the place to explain how and why these developments have taken place. Suffice it to say, several converging forces have, in combination, produced these tragic results. While our society was comfortably living off the legacy of a culture shaped largely by Christian conviction and truth, it was relatively easy for someone to reject Christianity yet enjoy its beneficial influence. As a crisis of authority emerged, bringing into question the basis on which right or wrong, true or false was determined, the result was an explosive war of cultures. The stress of these worldviews in conflict has caused considerable social upheaval and discomfort.[3] As a matter of fact, the conflict of cultures and worldviews has been experienced internationally and promises to be a major factor in world affairs during the twenty-first century.[4] In time these tensions will undoubtedly precipitate further change.

When our circumstances change enough to create some discomfort or when we realize that our usual responses no longer suffice, we then acknowledge the existence of a problem. At that point we are open to change and may even begin to question what we have always accepted. We look at information differently, perhaps seeing and hearing things we have not heard or seen before—though the information may have been there all along. At that point we are ready for a new solution or, as it is currently being called, "a new paradigm."

Faith and Knowledge

When the Holy Spirit works in your heart so that the gospel suddenly makes sense, you repent and believe. You become a new person with a new way of looking at life and a new motivation. Now, with the help of the Holy Spirit, you may begin to develop a new understanding of yourself and the world based on the explanation God provides in the Bible.

As his disciples, Christ expects us to grow in knowledge and wisdom in accordance with his truth. The word *disciple* actually means student or learner. Disciples, therefore, are students whose responsibility is to learn what God wants them to believe and how he wants them to live so that they may obey and honor him (Matt. 28:18–20). When Christians stagnate spiritually, failing to grow as expected, not only do they lose, but the entire church suffers. Those who have been Christians for a long time and have had ample opportunity to benefit from their knowledge and experience should have learned enough to be teachers. Unfortunately, many still need to master elementary matters (Heb. 5:11–14). Their prolonged spiritual immaturity is displeasing to the Lord. Milk may be a suitable diet for babies, but eventually their diet must become more substantial or their health and development will be impaired. Similarly, if Christians make no progress toward spiritual maturity, marked by well-developed knowledge and wisdom, the Lord will not be pleased.

This is a sensitive subject because the ignorance of most Christians is appalling, as has been well documented in recent years. They continue blissfully in their ignorance, quite unaware of its inevitable consequences. They do not sense a need to change, and they are uninterested in learning. It is far too easy to kick back and watch television.

Although the twentieth century witnessed a dismal failure of the church regarding its mandate to educate believers, my intent is not to ascribe blame. It is too late for that. Rather, we must acknowledge the current state of affairs. Just as it is difficult to think with an empty mind, so it is difficult to know what to believe and how to live without accurate biblical information and understanding. This being the case, it is important to chart a program for learning so that any believer who wishes may begin to learn in a systematic, comprehensive way the riches of truth in God's Word.

About the time I was completing my theological education, I was attracted to a delightful satire by the title *How to Become a Bishop without Being Religious*. As the budding young theologian listens to the advice of his mentor, he is warned to be careful about what he says because, he is cautioned, although 98 percent of the people would not know theological heresy if they ran into it, they would recognize social heresy immediately![5] Those words struck me as a powerful indictment against the church and its failure to teach Christians effectively during the last half of the twentieth century. Why can't people recognize theological heresy? Because we, the church, have not taught them. How have we failed? And why? Given the fact that we have expended so much energy in teaching and studying in evangelical churches, it is obvious that church members have not been learning in proportion to the time and energy expended in teaching them. When we don't achieve the results we are expecting, it is appropriate to ask why. This situation calls for a soul-searching critique of our failure. What can we do about it? How can we improve?

Back to the Basics

I am impressed with the way successful coaches in sports, music, and other fields emphasize the mastery of the basics as fundamental to achievement. Vince Lombardi, the legendary coach of the champion Green Bay Packers, used to begin training camp by assembling all the hardened, scarred veterans as well as the anxious green rookies in the training room. Holding a football in his stubby hand, he would give a menacing stare and bark in his gravelly deep voice, "Men, this is a football!" John Wooden, who coached the UCLA basketball team to an unprecedented seven national championships, would begin each season by reviewing basics such as how to tie your shoes! Such disciplined attention to basic details does not go unrewarded. Foundational instruction in every area of life is essential. Certainly, it is no less essential for the believer.

I can't say I enjoyed memorizing the multiplication tables or studying for spelling tests, but such tasks were essential to my education. The same can be said of my Christian "education." Soon after I became a Christian during my high school years, a pastor took interest in my spiritual nurturing and encouraged me to learn. Though I had learned little during my sporadic attendance at Sunday school prior

> There is no longer a Christian mind.
>
> Harry Blamires, *The Christian Mind*

to conversion, now I was motivated to read the Bible, study the Gospels, and memorize Scripture verses. Then my pastor directed my attention to substantial Christian literature, including the Westminster Shorter Catechism and the Westminster Confession of Faith. I had never heard of or seen these writings prior to this experience. Thus began my journey. To this day I am grateful for the direction and encouragement I received from a godly pastor who was willing to mentor and encourage a new Christian.

Thankfully, an abundance of good Christian literature is available. (See the suggested reading section). There is no excuse for failing to familiarize yourself with the edifying message of the Bible, centering on God's redemptive purpose in Christ. If you are serious about studying the Bible, you need to become acquainted with the purpose and basic outline of each book of the Bible. Next, you should learn what the Bible teaches about major subjects such as God, man, sin, Christ, salvation, the church, and the Christian life. These rudimentary truths are foundational to the development of a Christian mind. They will give you a structure or framework from which to work as you seek to grow and understand God's truth.

Beyond the Basics

As the author of Hebrews urges, however, you must press beyond this kind of elementary knowledge to a mature grasp of reality (Heb. 6:1). He refers to the basics, alluded to above, as foundational to growth toward maturity, but beyond these basic principles, there is much more to learn. Rather than merely accumulating additional information, whether profound or trivial, you need to learn how to relate all the material in meaningful ways so that you understand it and know what to do with it. Having the facts is one thing; knowing how to apply them is another.

That does not lessen the value of knowing the facts. It is difficult to think with an empty mind. You need to know or have access to necessary information before you can apply it. People who have steel-trap memories impress me, and there is something to be said for cultivating this ability, whether to memorize Scripture or for other purposes. There was a time when biblical teachers committed vast portions of Scripture to memory. At one point in history, it was said that any twelve rabbis assembled together could recite the entire Old Testament. Impressive, to say the least! We have lost something of value by failing to store Scripture and other important Christian truth in our memory banks.

One of the serendipities of my life has been frequent contact and association with intelligent people. The mental quickness and sheer brilliance of some scholars is dazzling. It is absolutely amazing to observe someone who is gifted in this way and note how penetrating and precise their thought processes can be—or their ability to comprehend and synthesize technical or highly theoretical material. On the other hand, give some of them a simple, practical task that would be considered routine for a child, and they can fall flat on their faces! It is occasionally humorous, but it also serves as a reminder of the importance of knowing how to relate information usefully in all areas of life.

I recall a remarkably gifted friend who was a walking encyclopedia. No one came close to matching his mastery of data, much of it trivial. Ask how many square miles are in the Atlantic Ocean or the capital city of any country, and he knew it. Ask the average temperature of a region during the year, and he could tell you. His information bin seemed bottomless. In addition, he spoke two languages from his youth. During junior high school, we spent lots of time together and he taught me how to play chess. Soon after, he won a National Science Foundation Award for a three-dimensional chess game he developed. By our senior year in high school, he was in the top percentile of all state and national testing and had received a full scholarship to the Massachusetts Institute of Technology. He was intelligent; more than that, he was brilliant. But he was different! His peers would have dubbed him "weird." The routine, ordinary experiences of life often escaped him. Sometimes brilliant people are like that. His intelligence was directed to certain areas, primarily academic, and did not function equally in other areas of his life. He easily misjudged people and found it difficult to establish and maintain relationships. Being smart doesn't make you wise. He taught me that.

The Need for Wisdom

By contrast, wisdom addresses the breadth and complexity of life, relating Scripture accurately to every aspect of human experience. Wise people take the principles and priorities of the Bible and apply them to given circumstances in an appropriate way. Once you accurately analyze your situation in its context, you must relate it to your analysis of scriptural teaching. This is more difficult than it may seem because life is complex. Although life may contain general patterns, each situation is unique, requiring an ability to analyze it from various perspectives, noting all facets and seeing how they relate. Such wisdom is a mark of spiritual maturity.

In some instances, the Bible speaks directly and forcefully to an issue at hand. The commandments are a good example: Do not murder; do not commit adultery; do not steal; and do not covet (Exod. 20:13–17). In other instances, the Bible provides the raw material from which, after thoughtful analysis, we must arrive at a final action or decision that will honor the Lord:

Should I marry?
Whom should I marry?
How should we raise our children?
How many children should we have?
How should I choose my vocation?
How should I decide where to live?
How should I invest my money?
How should I vote?

The Bible does not give direct answers to these and many similar questions, but it does provide the basic information needed for us to arrive at answers. To do so, we need to understand and harmonize the principles and priorities of Scripture into a frame of reference that gives meaning to life and provides the basis on which such decisions can be made. This frame of reference is a set of collected convictions about reality that represents a person's outlook on life. It is sometimes called a worldview or philosophy of life.[6]

The Puritans were good at painstakingly and thoroughly applying the Bible to life. William Law, the eighteenth-century Puritan writer, put it this way in his book, *A Serious Call to a Devout and Holy Life:*

> The more we discover God in everything, the more we seek him in every place, the more we look up to him in all our actions, the more we conform to his will, the more we act according to his wisdom and imitate his goodness, so much the more we enjoy God. Then we share in the divine nature and heighten and increase all that is happy and comfortable in human life.[7]

The cumulative achievement of the Puritans, built on the contribution of earlier Christians, by and large determined the value system that prevailed well into this century. We have lived off that legacy for many generations, taking it for granted and seldom appreciating its full value.

During the last third of the twentieth century that worldview was sharply challenged and rejected by a rising generation and is disintegrating at an alarming pace. The highly publicized culture wars of our most recent past underscore the catastrophic changes that are occurring.

We live in a period of social turbulence and moral upheaval. Life is unraveling quickly, which is extremely unsettling, but it is difficult to find anyone with the ability to move beyond merely reacting to major issues and to build a constructive approach to life. The challenge for Christians is to put life back together again so that it makes sense and glorifies God. The unity and connectedness of life as created by God should lead us to a coherent understanding so that no matter what we do, no matter how seemingly unimportant or inconsequential it may be, it can fulfill the purpose of serving and pleasing the Lord. The ultimate purpose of the transformed life is to reflect the character of God, including his infinite wisdom. When this happens, people will begin to realize that our understanding of life is different from theirs. Why we think or behave differently may elude them, but they will become aware that we are different as they observe us and listen to our conversations.

By now it should be clear that Christianity should lead us to a different way of viewing all of life—a worldview. No vocation, no action, no detail is excluded when you

> Except over a very narrow field of thinking chiefly touching questions of strictly personal conduct, we Christians in the modern world accept, for the purpose of mental activity, a frame of reference constructed by the secular mind and a set of criteria reflecting secular evolutions.
>
> Harry Blamires, *The Christian Mind*

develop such a biblically informed philosophy of life. The challenge is to develop a Christian mind. It isn't easy to do. It requires hard work and serious thought. Memorizing a few Bible verses and mastering several outlines will not suffice, helpful though it may be to do so. To give you an idea, approximately 25 percent of all American adults claim their worldview is based on biblical principles, yet less than one out of ten from that group, when asked, could explain their worldview or how they developed it.[8]

If you are serious about attaining spiritual maturity, you may not neglect this responsibility. Yet getting believers to realize this and apply themselves has proven difficult. As a result, most Americans, including Christians, "do not have an intentionally developed Christian worldview, but they have become comfortable with the way things are" and are not interested in changing.[9] Yet the failure to achieve a Christian worldview that is widely understood and embraced is costly, as we have seen from the swift collapse of the prevailing worldview during the last third of the twentieth century. The prophetic warning of the former Secretary General of the United Nations, Dr. Charles Malik, must become our watchword in the twenty-first century: "If you win the whole world and lose the mind of the world, you will soon discover you have not won the world you have actually lost the world."[10]

A Christian Approach to Eating

As you may recall, idolatry was a prevalent practice in the ancient world, and it often proved to be a sensitive issue for newly converted Christians. They wanted to break with their past and not compromise their newfound faith. They also did not want to confuse those they were trying to reach evangelistically by appearing to remain linked in any way to idolatrous practices. So when, as the guests of others or in a public venue, they were invited to eat meat that had been offered to idols, they found themselves faced with a dilemma. Should they eat the meat or not? They had to make a wise decision.

The meat was safe to eat. That was not the issue. The problem was the perception of the unbelievers who were present. If Christians erected unnecessary barriers between themselves and the unbelievers they hoped to evangelize by declaring that they could not eat meat offered to idols, they could impair their witness. On the other hand, someone could point out that the meat had been offered to idols, thereby testing the Christians to see whether they would follow Christian principles. To eat the meat under those circumstances would be a mistake and mar their testimony.

In explaining to the Corinthian Christians how they should think about idolatry as it related to food, Paul made a number of important points including, "Everything is permissible—but not everything is beneficial. Everything is permissible—but not everything is constructive. Nobody should seek his own good, but the good of others" (1 Cor. 10:23–24). He sought to help them think through what food they should or should not eat and also what they should do in other similar situations. During his explanation he urged, "So whether you eat or drink or whatever you do, do it all for the glory of God" (1 Cor. 10:31; cf. Col. 3:17). His principal concern, whether in regard to food or other matters, was, How do you glorify God and keep the door open to reach as many people as possible with the gospel (1 Cor. 9:1–6, 19–23)?

Following up on Paul's statement, it is still valuable to ask, How do you eat to the glory of God? Although eating food sacrificed to idols is not a current issue, eating to God's glory should be. Few people contemplate that question, and if you were to ask someone that question, he or she would probably respond, "How does eating affect spirituality or wisdom in any significant way?" It is obvious that Paul meant for his admonition to be taken seriously, though we may concede that most people would not think it to be worth the effort. Although it is necessary to eat to live, apart from weight and health concerns, people give little thought to this matter. Yet, as the historian Paul Johnson chides, "Considering how large a part of our life we spend eating, and how vital it is to our existence, we devote surprisingly little attention to thinking seriously and systematically about it."[11] When you stop to think about it, it is difficult to justify a neglect of something that is such a necessity. This is especially true when you acknowledge that it has significant spiritual ramifications.

A recent article in *The Chronicle of Higher Education* called attention to the research being done by Yong Chen of the University of California at Irvine. He plans to write a book about the political, cultural, and economic significance of food traditions, which he views as carriers of social memory and ethnicity. He notes that food in many cultures "is as important as religion. That's why dieting laws in numerous religions tell us what we can and cannot eat."[12] In light of this information, perhaps we should become more reflective about our eating habits and other time-consuming activities. We may in the process discover far more than we would expect regarding our underlying assumptions as well as the difference that certain principles can make in regard to routine activities.

If you want to learn how to eat to the glory of God, you must first ascertain the biblical principles that apply to eating. Let me suggest several for your consideration.

Prayer

A Christian should pause to pray, giving thanks to God for his provision of the food before eating (1 Tim. 4:3–5). The prayer of thanksgiving before a meal is an acknowledgment of dependence on the Lord for our daily needs, including our food. When we receive such gifts, God deserves our thanks and praise for his generous and gracious provision.

What You Eat

What you eat is important because your body is the temple of the Holy Spirit. The commandment "do not kill" also underscores the sanctity of life. Therefore, we are obligated to take care of our bodies so that they will last and be of service (Exod. 20:13; 1 Cor. 3:16; 6:19). Therefore, we should eat healthy, nutritious foods conducive to good health. We should also be concerned about the preparation and condition of the food we eat to ensure its maximum benefit. Fortunately, we have sufficient choices and can, for the most part, eat food that not only is good for us but also appeals to our palates.

On the opposite side of the coin, we need to avoid items that are detrimental to good health. While medical research has frustratingly reversed its conclusions in regard to various foods and drinks, it remains clear that some items are bad for your health. Obviously, this is true of drugs and narcotics such as cocaine. But excessive amounts

> I do not try, Lord, to obtain your lofty heights, because my understanding is in no way equal to it. But I do desire to understand your truth a little, that truth that my heart believes and loves. For I do not seek to understand so that I may believe; but I believe so that I may understand. For I believe this also, that "unless I believe I shall not understand."
>
> St. Anselm, *Proslogiom*

of junk food high in salt and fat can also negatively influence weight and health. We also know that certain vitamin deficiencies cause health problems, as surely as sailors learned years ago that the absence of certain nutrients caused scurvy. One dearly loved friend who developed colon cancer was told by her doctors that less fast foods and more fruits and vegetables in her diet could have reduced the likelihood of this disease. It is also worth mentioning the damage that certain foods or beverages can cause. The lives ruined and sometimes ended by alcohol abuse is one poignant example. A plethora of literature on the subject of food and health is available for Christians to read as they contemplate eating to the glory of God.

How Much You Eat

Third, if what you eat makes a difference, so does how much you eat. We are well aware of the health problems caused by overeating, as well as by eating too little. Eating disorders are serious problems that must be addressed as early as possible, preferably through professional help. The current emphasis on the appearance of the body, especially among girls and women, has led many of them to injure their health by eating too little. The preponderance of Americans, on the other hand, tend to eat too much and are overweight. It is possible to err in either direction, but it is an incontrovertible fact that how much we eat makes a difference as we honor God (see Phil. 3:19; Titus 1:12).

We must remember that the body is the temple of the Holy Spirit. As we strive to live in a way that honors our bodies and pleases God, we need to exercise discernment and discipline to find a path between gluttony and anorexia. It is easy to cross the line into troublesome territory. I love to eat, and I hate to see food wasted, so I can easily become the family garbage can. But my metabolism is not what it was in younger more active days, so it would be a mistake to give in to the urge. I also remember a friend who gained eighty pounds during her first pregnancy. She ate to comfort herself. One day she described a visit to the doctor's office for a routine checkup. The doctor told her she was gaining too much weight. My friend was so upset she went right out and ordered a hot fudge sundae to console herself. Her short-term remedy—turning to food for comfort—brought long-term misery.

How You Eat

Fourth, how you eat also matters. As a child I detested some rules of the dinner table that I was forced to observe. I must admit, to this day, some of them still seem senseless to me! Still, we must realize that deportment and etiquette communicate something important. For example, learning to wait for your host or hostess to begin eating before you dig in, placing a napkin in your lap, learning to pass the food, and many other gestures at the table make a difference. As those who are made and are being remade in the image of God, we affirm the dignity and value of each person. That dignity and worth must be reflected in all activities, including how we eat. Perhaps Leon Kass, in his chapter on sanctified eating, has a point when he insists, "Even when dining alone, and—let me push the point—even were he or she the last human being on earth eating the last meal, the virtuous human being would cover and set the table, use the implements properly, and would chew noiselessly with mouth closed."[13]

Recently I heard someone say, "We are civilized here so we don't do that." Being civilized does make a difference; it differentiates us from those who have no such concerns. This was driven home to me some years ago while watching the highly regarded film *Lion in Winter*. As it began, the camera panned across a forbidding, foggy marsh to the

> The greatness of wisdom, which is nothing if not of God, is invisible to the carnal-minded and to intellectuals.
>
> Blaise Pascal, *Pensées*

ominous gray-walled fortress, then slipped inside to reveal a regal banquet in the great dining hall of the castle. The king and his companions, however, were anything but regal in appearance and behavior. Boisterous banqueters stuffed food in their mouths with their bare hands and swilled wine so greedily that it ran down their chins and necks. Dogs ran around under the table gobbling up everything that fell or dribbled onto the floor. The "regal" guests at the banquet behaved more like animals than humans. Toward the end of the movie that behavior was acknowledged by the king, who said to his queen, "We are not much more than animals, are we?" A telling remark. But we know that we are not brute animals! We are much more. We are image bearers of God and must reflect the dignity of our being and our relationship to God in all areas, including how we eat.

Aesthetic Factors

God is the author of beauty as well as of truth. Given this, the appearance of what we eat as well as the setting in which we eat may be seen in a different light. I recall eating a meal under less than desirable circumstances. Construction was under way in an adjacent room, and next to

> The myth sovereign in the old age was that everything means everything. The myth sovereign in the new age is that nothing means anything.
>
> **Thomas Howard,** *Chance or the Dance*

our table, through a large hole in the wall, we could see a huge pile of garbage, some of it food. Flies and other insects hovered over it and then visited our table. There was no air conditioning, and although the smells were not too disconcerting, I couldn't help but think about the unsanitary conditions and the potential of becoming ill as a result. For some reason, my appetite deserted me that day.

On the other hand, I vividly remember a dinner in an elegant restaurant. Each table held fresh flowers and was attractively set with fine china and silver. A string ensemble played softly from the far side of the room. A courteous waiter in a tuxedo with a crisply starched white shirt and black tie awaited our direction. The meal, in every detail, was magnificent; the presentation of each course was stunning. It was a memorable evening. There is no doubt that attention to the aesthetic aspect of eating is important. Do we pay enough attention to aesthetic factors in our daily meal presentation? It does make a difference.[14]

Economic Factors

The cost of a meal should also be taken into consideration since all of life relates to stewardship. That being so, you should evaluate the cost of a meal relative to your monthly budget and specifically your budget for food. The occasion for the meal and its participants are also factors. If the meal is for a special occasion with guests, it will more than likely cost more because it is extraordinary. Likewise, an occasional meal out for a family with limited resources may be worth more than its cost to the mother whose daily responsibilities of cooking, cleaning, and maintaining the home seldom provide her with a respite. Factors such as these must be taken into consideration when seeking to honor God.

Consideration of Others

Finally, what effect will the above factors have on other people? More than likely, serving snails, eels, or perhaps squid to your guests for dinner would make an indelible impression, though not the one you intended (although in some countries and among some ethnic groups it would be customary to serve such delicacies). If you host a meal in such a way that it makes your guests uncomfortable or is an unpleasant experience, whether by serving an unknown food or an undesirable dish, using few manners, or behaving like a glutton, the occasion of eating becomes a burden not a delight. Once as a young boy visiting relatives, I was forced to eat something I detested—liver. (A huge slab of it too!) I did as required, perhaps I should say coerced, but to this day, I remember that unpleasant experience and how it made me feel. It has made me more sensitive about pressing any guest to try something when they initially decline. Although one incident surely will not permanently affect your relationship to your hosts, it can affect your perception of their sensitivity and concern for your welfare. Similarly, you might ask how the total experience at a meal affects those who join you, including their perception of you and your values (1 Cor. 10:31).

Undoubtedly, you could think of other factors that could be considered when seeking a Christian approach to eating. These examples, however, should give you an idea of how to think about this topic in light of biblical teaching. Hopefully, this discussion has also shown you that no area of life is outside a Christian worldview or beyond the application of wisdom.

Worldview Wisdom

A worldview consciously or unconsciously informs all our thoughts and actions, even mundane matters such as eating, housecleaning, driving a car, and mowing the grass. Biblical principles rather than secular principles should shape our worldview because all of life is to be directed to the glory of God. To relegate the influence of Christianity to nothing more than church-related matters or overtly spiritual activities and to live the rest of life as if it were free from Christian obligation or direction is a serious mistake. Your faith should be expressed in all the details of life. It should affect all that you are and all that you do. The beautiful words penned by the English hymn writer Katie Wilkinson express it well:

> May the mind of Christ my Savior
> Live in me from day to day,
> By his love and power controlling
> All I do and say.

118

May his beauty rest upon me
As I seek the lost to win,
And may they forget the channel,
Seeing only him.

The task is to blend everything into one unified, coherent whole. This does not have to be a self-conscious activity every time we do something. No one has enough time for that. Over time, however, putting Christian wisdom into practice becomes a habitual activity, like driving a car or reading a paper. The first few times you drove a car you were self-conscious about every small detail. In time, that awkwardness subsided and driving became routine. The same can be said of living to the glory of God. However, you must first develop the skills and know how to measure your behavior and thinking against Scripture before you can become effective and wise in serving the Lord.

A perennial mistake is the division of life into sacred and secular. You may recall the film *Chariots of Fire*, which celebrated the life and testimony of Eric Liddell, an Olympic champion. At one point his sister Jenny complained about the amount of time he spent running. To her, it seemed a waste of time. Surely he had far more important things to do. In her opinion, he might better have spent that time in specifically Christian ministry. Eric's response was that God made him to run, and when he did so, he gave God pleasure. His was the more biblical response. As he recognized that God had given him an unusual ability to run fast and utilized that ability, he honored God. Jenny, on the other hand, was like the person who says you must be in "full-time" ministry to truly honor the Lord.

According to this kind of thinking, profoundly spiritual people are missionaries, ministers, or other full-time Christian ministry employees. It is not unusual to encounter people who have recently become Christians and are persuaded that to serve God they must enter "the ministry." This view, however, is misguided. It reminds me of a friend who fumed and fussed following a budget meeting. "Did you see how much they are spending on administration and how little is left for the Lord's work?" Although his

> It is said that ideas have consequences, and this is undoubtedly true. Still it seems that the ideas with the most profound consequences are frequently taken for granted. They are the ideas that lie just behind conscious thought, providing a kind of foundation for the deliberations of everyday life. They are the ideas that define the way things are and demarcate the possibilities of life.
>
> Craig Gay, *The Way of the (Modern) World*

concern about the percentage consumed by administration may have been legitimate, he was ignoring the fact that administrators serve the Lord too. To have organizational structure and planned activities is not outside "the Lord's work."

Obviously, I am not opposed to persuading people to become missionaries or pastors or to hold other positions of service in the church or in Christian organizations. These are wonderful and blessed callings. But we must also acknowledge that every vocation—unless it involves intentional sinful activity—is a Christian vocation. We need more wise Christians in all vocations—politics, media, business, education. God calls all believers to be ministers wherever we are, for we are "a royal priesthood" (1 Peter 2:9). We must serve the Lord diligently and conscientiously wherever we are and in whatever we do. Nothing less will suffice. The businessman, doctor, homemaker, or educator serves God—or may serve God—just as much as any pastor. These are not lesser, inferior vocations spiritually.

The Benefits of Wisdom

What are the benefits of true knowledge and wisdom built on Scripture with the help of the Holy Spirit? One of the immediate benefits is that actions and decisions flow from a unified, integrated understanding of God and life. Meaning and coherence are connected. Given the fragmentation and disconnectedness of life, including our atomistic, fragmented approach to education in the Western world, the person who "has it together," so to speak, is wise.

The Bible says a wise person develops discernment or the ability to tell right from wrong and truth from falsehood (Heb. 5:14), or as Paul puts it, "Then we will no longer be infants, tossed back and forth by the waves, and blown here and there by every wind of teaching and by the cunning and craftiness of men in their deceitful scheming" (Eph. 4:14). Who wants to be a fool? Who wants to waste time, energy, or money on wrong and fruitless causes? Who wants to be duped into supporting evil people or causes? It is difficult to forget that sick feeling and hard knot in your stomach when you discover a mistake you made that could have been easily avoided had you been wise or taken the advice of a wise person. To have discernment, not to be fooled by every new trend or idea that comes along, is valuable, as is the ability to detect telltale clues in given situations that let you know what to do. It is like the golfer who knows the right club to select for a shot or how to read the green before directing his putt (see Prov. 1:1–7).

Wisdom also brings stability because you are able to make decisions and take actions that keep you on course. Avoiding distraction on the one hand and deceit on the other assures stability. When the storms of life come, bringing pain and hardship, testing and trying, as they inevitably do, the mature, wise Christian stands firmly planted on the truth while the efforts of the foolish person are swept away (Matt. 7:24–27).

Strong, wise, stable people can be relied upon in every kind of situation. When trouble strikes, they seldom fail. If you were to face a difficult life-changing decision and needed counsel, to whom would you turn? To a mature, wise Christian, if at all possible. Such people are the true pillars of the church. We expect and want them to be our leaders. I am blessed to have a family friend who is an older, godly lady with far-reaching wisdom. It is a blessing to seek her advice and counsel and to enjoy the benefits of her life experiences.

God wants you to become a mature, wise person who will be a blessing to others and a testimony to his grace, and you can be as you press toward the goal of your high calling in Christ, becoming more like the one in whom is hidden all the fullness of wisdom and knowledge. It will, however, require discipline and work on your part to achieve that wisdom, so commit yourself to lifelong learning as his disciple.

QUESTIONS FOR REFLECTION

1. What is a Christian worldview?
2. How would you explain God's wisdom?
3. How do you work to the glory of God?
4. Are there areas in your life that need to be more consistent with your faith? What can you do to make this happen?
5. Name three people you would identify as wise and explain why.

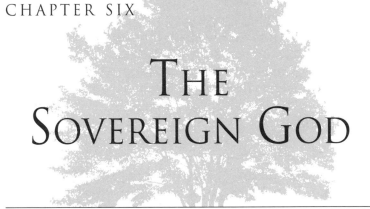

CHAPTER SIX

THE
SOVEREIGN GOD

HIS KINGDOM ENDURES FROM GENERATION TO GENERATION.

DANIEL 4:34

In his first volume of *Children of Crisis,* Robert Coles quotes a young Mississippian: "The Lord made me. When I grow up, my mama says I may not like how He made me, but I must always remember that He did it and it's His idea. So when I draw the Lord, He'll be a real big man. He has to be to explain the way things are."[1]

The truth is, God is big, all-powerful, and all-knowing. He is the sovereign God, the maker and ruler of this universe. Sinful human nature would make him small, control his power, determine what he thinks and permits, so that he becomes palatable to us, allowing us to think and live as we wish—with his blessing, of course (Rom. 1:22–23, 25). No wonder God commands so little respect

123

and life moves on relatively unchanged in our secular world. But let unbelievers say or think what they will—denying and defying him. He is in control, and one day everyone will have to give him an account.

God is great! We need to recover that biblical sense of the greatness and majesty of God for our time with attendant feelings of reverence and awe. When we do, we shall discover the huge implications for our lives. Consider, therefore, what the Bible tells us about the greatness of God.

God spoke and the cosmos materialized from nothing. That a mere word brought the universe into being is almost inconceivable. But for the omnipotent God it was not challenging—creative, yes, but a strain, no (Pss. 33:5–9; 148:5). With him, nothing is too difficult or impossible (Job 42:2; Mark 14:36). Whatever he wishes happens, and nothing occurs except as he wills it. Thomas à Kempis rightly observed that "man proposes, but God disposes." God's awesome power, displayed spectacularly in creation, remains our guarantee that he is able to sustain this universe.

> The heavens declare thy glory, Lord:
> In every star thy goodness shines;
> But when our eyes behold thy word
> We read thy name in fairer lines.

> Isaac Watts, Psalm 19[2]

The Bible reveals God's awareness of every detail, stating that he knows the number of hairs on your head and not even a sparrow can die without his knowledge (Luke 12:6–7). He causes the sun to rise and sends the rain, which is a picturesque biblical way of saying that all natural phenomena are under his providential control. Even insurance companies refer to an earthquake or similar event as an act of God. It is a matter of hands-on control of the universe, according to J. I. Packer, who observes, "His hand may be hidden but his rule is absolute."[3]

Following the flood, by which God brought a destructive judgment on the world during Noah's life, God promised that he would not repeat that cataclysmic judgment and placed a rainbow in the sky as a reminder of his promise. In addition, he promised to maintain the steady rhythm of the seasons. "As long as the earth endures, seedtime and harvest, cold and heat, summer and winter, day and night will never cease" (Gen. 8:22). What we refer to as the laws of nature are evidence of his continued prov-

> Yours, O LORD, is the greatness and the power
>   and the glory and the majesty and the splendor,
>   for everything in heaven and on earth is yours.
> Yours, O LORD, is the kingdom;
>   you are exalted as Lord over all.
> Wealth and honor come from you;
>   you are the ruler of all things.
> In your hands are strength and power
>   to exalt and give strength to all.
> Now, Our God, we give you thanks,
>   and praise your glorious name.
>
> 1 Chronicles 29:11–13

idential governance. Without his steadying hand, we could not be sure that the sun would rise, that an apple dropped would fall to the ground, or that heat would rise. Each day we witness the constant evidence of his orderly rule of the universe. The psalmist concludes, "These all look to you to give them their food at the proper time" (Ps. 104:27; cf. vv. 5, 8–14). The apostle Paul said, "For from him and through him and to him are all things. To him be the glory forever" (Rom. 11:36; see also 1 Cor. 8:6).

God's absolute, sovereign power is unmistakably demonstrated by his providential control of this world as he sustains and preserves it. The connection between creation and providence was underscored by John Calvin:

Herein lies the unfathomable greatness of God . . . not only did He once create heaven and earth but He also guides the whole process according to His will. Thus he who confesses God as creator while supposing He remains tranquilly in heaven without caring for the world, outrageously deprives God of all effective power.[4]

Although his ways are not our ways, nor his thoughts our thoughts, because they are higher than ours (Isa. 55:8–9), nevertheless, we can be sure that because he rules and because no one can prevent him from doing what he intends, all things will work out well for his beloved people, the community of faith. Our security as well as our hope are inextricably tied to his sovereign power. We cannot experience any assurance regarding our future unless he actually has all power and controls human history. How else could we discover any assurance or security? What would be the source? Who would want to accept blind chance as a preferred alternative to the benevolent providence of God?

The Cultural Mandate

When God created Adam and Eve in his image, he gave them a mandate to subdue the earth (Gen. 1:28). His own sovereign rule was assumed in his appointment of them as his delegates to rule creation. This was an essential part of their nature and became their responsibility as the only godlike creatures in all the universe. Psalm 8:4–8 states it clearly:

> what is man that you are mindful of him,
>   the son of man that you care for him?
> You made him a little lower than the heavenly beings
>   and crowned him with glory and honor.
> You made him ruler over the works of your hands;

> you put everything under his feet:
> all flocks and herds,
>   and the beasts of the field,
> the birds of the air,
>   and the fish of the sea,
>   all that swim the paths of the seas.

The concept of rulership is connected in the strongest possible way with the idea of the image of God, according to Old Testament scholar D. J. A. Caines, who contends that any definition of the image of God in man that does not refer to rulership is deficient.[5] In this capacity, Adam represents the kingship or lordship of God to the rest of God's creation.

What was expected of Adam and Eve in response to the directive "fill the earth and subdue it" (Gen. 1:28)? The mandate should be seen as more than an ambiguously delegated responsibility and authority. In assuming the responsible stewardship of the Lord's magnificent creation, they had a unique opportunity to embellish and enrich it. They were expected to have a direct positive influence on all of creation. They could influence plant and animal life by harnessing them harmoniously and productively in the Lord's service so that through their concerted effort all of the resources at their disposal could be directed to the glory of God. The rich potential of God's Word could be realized through their attentive, guiding influence.

The tragedy is that their disobedience shattered that possibility. How often after their banishment do you think they wondered about what might have been if they had only obeyed God's admonition? They were left instead to deal with the brutal realities of their new circumstances. When they endeavored to subdue the earth, they now found resistance rather than compliant cooperation. The task of producing food became difficult work, made more unpleasant by thorns and thistles. When they had additional children to share the burden, pain was mixed with pleasure, both in the birth and training of their children.

Throughout human history, this struggle has continued. Often in their desire to extract the full potential of the land, people have raped it instead, destroying its rich, productive capacity. Consider North Africa, once the breadbasket of the world, or the difficult lessons learned in the United States following the decimation of virgin forests and wildlife, such as the buffalo.

The Desire for Power and Influence

The drive to influence, organize, and rule that was innate with Adam began to express itself in various ways as people imposed their wills on others—sometimes to influence an outcome or fulfill a desire, at other times to subjugate people. When Joseph's brothers became tired of him and the special treatment they felt he received from their father, they physically assaulted him, then sold him to slave traders (Gen. 37:18–28). He was an unwanted irritant, so they got rid of him. When Potiphar's wife was unable to lure Joseph into bed, she falsely accused him, and her husband had him thrown into prison (Gen. 39:6–20). When David saw Bathsheba, he wanted her so badly that he arranged to have her husband, Uriah, placed at such a prominent position in battle that he would inevitably be killed (2 Sam. 11:2–27).

The imposition of one's will on others assumed gargantuan proportions as kings rose to power, then attempted to enlarge their kingdoms by conquering other nations. Rulers made war to increase their power, as Hitler did in the twentieth century. History is replete with examples of coercion, manipulation, and deceit to gain power. Given this context, it is easy to understand why some non-

Christians view life as a selfish quest for power and influence and are concerned, therefore, to determine the real agenda in any given situation. No matter how successful some efforts to obtain power and glory may be, the inevitable result is captured well by Percy Shelley in his poem "Ozymandias":

> I met a traveler from an antique land who said:
> Two vast and trunkless legs of stone
> Stand in the desert. Near them, on the sand,
> Half sunk, a shattered visage lies, whose frown,
> And wrinkled lip, and sneer of cold command,
> Tell that its sculptor well those passions read
> And on the pedestal these words appear:
> "My name is Ozymandias, king of kings:
> Look at my works, ye Mighty and despair!"
> Nothing beside remains. Round the decay
> Of that colossal wreck, boundless and bare
> The lone and level sands stretch far away.[6]

The Power of the Gospel

The power of the gospel lies in the fact that Jesus' kingdom is not of this world. Jesus told Peter to put away his sword (John 18:10–11), and he taught his disciples that grasping for titles and power is inappropriate (Mark 10:35–45). Jesus himself gave up the regal prerogatives of heaven and became a human being like us for our salvation. When the devil tempted him with an offer of all the kingdoms of this world, Christ quickly rejected the offer (Matt. 4:8–10). He had already given up those benefits for us when he came to serve and to lay down his life for our redemption (Mark 10:45). He allowed himself to be subjected to the wicked power of Rome and the Sanhedrin, a power they intended to use to destroy him and his influence. Then, when Jesus had accomplished his mission, making atonement for our sins, he rose from the grave victoriously. Having now conquered sin, death, and the grave, he ascended to the right hand of the Father, where he holds all power and authority. Because he willingly abandoned any claim to title or power, he has been exalted to the highest place possible and given a name above every name so "that at the name of Jesus every knee should bow in heaven and on earth" (Phil. 2:10).

The believer who desires to be like Christ soon realizes that Christ's way is to serve, not to be served; it is to be self-effacing, not to press for fame and recognition; it is to

> The great challenge here is faithfulness, which must be lived in the choices of every moment. When your eating, drinking, working, playing, speaking, or writing is no longer for the glory of God, you should stop it immediately, because you no longer live for the glory of God, you begin living for your own glory. Then you separate yourself from God and do yourself harm.
>
> Henri Nouwen, *The Inner Voice*

accept quietly the last place rather than boorishly shove your way to the front (Matt. 20:25–27). When you humble yourself, relinquishing a claim to power or influence, acknowledging your weakness, you discover a higher, greater power (2 Cor. 12:9–10). When the Lord is ready, he will elevate you. If, in the community of faith, your service proves beneficial and edifying, you will be given greater opportunity and influence. But if you grasp for power or influence, though you do so with the best of intentions, you align yourself with the unbelieving world, not with the Lord, for he warned against lording it over others (Mark 10:42–43; 1 Peter 5:3). He does not approve of domineering controllers who try to conceal their true motives behind smiling faces and pious words.

The Cultural Mandate and Spirituality

For the believer being remade in the image of God, the cultural mandate takes on a new redemptive significance. Called to exercise dominion in a world resistant to it—a world of disruption, chaos, and evil—the challenge is to bring order and direction as God's stewards who must one day give an account to him for what we have done with the resources placed at our disposal (Matt. 25:14–30). Life is a stewardship. We must make the most of it because we will one day be judged by it.

The stewardship of life does not receive adequate attention and emphasis. If our stewardship is directly related to our final accountability to God, then it must become a consuming passion, giving purpose and focus to all our efforts. This can and probably should be understood primarily in terms of personal responsibility and achievement. We are responsible to assess our gifts and our opportunities as they relate to the needs around us, then concentrate our efforts, in dependence on the Lord, on accomplishing as much as we can. Squandering resources and opportunities to serve and glorify the Lord is irresponsible.

Admittedly, it is difficult to determine a course of action that will result in the best stewardship possible. That is why wisdom is required to make such decisions in a complex world. The use of acquired wisdom in the exercise of our wills is a mark of our likeness to God. Spiritual maturity brings a closer alignment between our will and God's as we, as his stewards, try to serve him.

God makes each person unique, and each person is influenced by his or her nationality, education, location, financial situation, and so on. The child of God discerns in his or her gifts, circumstances, and the influence of the Holy Spirit a call to serve the Lord. From the earliest days of my new life as a Christian, I keenly felt the push to use my life wisely to serve the Lord. Decisions were sometimes difficult, but that was because the weight of responsibility and accountability was real. The more concerned you are about pleasing God through the stewardship of your life, the more this influences your decisions and life choices.

Choosing a vocation is one such life choice. Once you make a decision, it is important to organize and manage the affairs of your life to accomplish that vocational calling. Your education, experiences, and associations will all in some way relate to the fulfillment of your calling. You must, therefore, remain alert and attempt to note the significance of each and make the most of it, disciplining yourself to remain focused on what you want to accomplish. Often it is the person who perseveres by faith through thick and thin, refusing to become distracted, who accomplishes the most. I recall one highly successful businessman who did just that. He was smart, and he carefully reviewed strategic opportunities before making decisions. But to him, the real key was "keeping on keeping on" once he determined his life's direction.

Spiritually mature believers who are concerned about the stewardship of life also attempt to organize and manage personal life, family life, the church, business, and government. Our Christian responsibility calls us to order each area to glorify God. It will not happen by itself; we must try to influence all areas of life so that they will be pleasing to the Lord. The stewardship of each of these facets of life is no less a spiritual responsibility than participation in church activities such as worship.

Paul compared the Christian life to a race that required "strict training" and did not allow him to "run like a man running aimlessly" (1 Cor. 9:25–27). While pleasure and frivolity are not bad, if done to excess they can rob you of worthwhile achievement. A mature believer seeks balance to be productive. Who wants to conclude late in life that most of it has been wasted, foolishly frittered away?

Of all sad words of tongue or pen
The saddest are these, it might have been.

John Greenleaf Whittier, "Maud Muller"[7]

Stewardship and Creation

Spiritual maturity also reflects a concern for the stewardship of the created world. In terms of material resources, we are responsible to preserve and protect what God has given. That is one conclusion we can make from the cultural mandate. It is buttressed by the repetitive refrain "it is good" as God's assessment of his creation. Because the creation is good as the handiwork of God, we are under an obligation to recognize that and respond accordingly. If we deface or corrupt something good, then we are at fault. Because God's creation is good, we must attempt to prevent any deterioration of what is good and find creative and constructive ways to enhance it. We may not ignore the created world because we are supposed to use and improve it.

Unfortunately, as the global population has swollen to nearly six billion people, pollution has become a major problem, as has the waste created by industrial production as well as the sheer enormity of the population. We are obligated to keep what we have clean and usable. Just as a campsite should be restored after using it, so the appearance and quality of our land, water, and air need to be kept clean and reusable. If we are concerned about the water we drink but neglect the water that the fish and animals use, we have failed in our stewardship. The principle here is the preservation and continued productive usefulness of all resources.

God has endowed his creation with a marvelous ability to renew and replenish itself. If we, for whatever reason, destroy or diminish that ability of the earth, we are in conflict with God's purpose. Moreover, the Lord has also created a remarkable balance in the created world that enables the world to sustain itself. It is interesting to observe how running water can purify itself within a short distance unless toxic additions are present as a result of human activity. The food chain is another example. If through excessive use of pesticides or hunting an animal such as the wolf is eliminated, then the various animals on which wolves feed may multiply rapidly and cause other problems. Upsetting the balance causes problems and goes against God's desire for creation.

The stewardship of natural resources surely includes the need to produce enough food to meet the needs of the population. This is not a hurdle in the United States, since now barely 2 percent of the population is able to produce all the food that is consumed. At the same time, however, the mature Christian steward needs to consider the effects of pesticides and fertilizers that have made this abundant food production possible. As is now well established, pesticides used for controlling insects and plant disease may in themselves cause other problems. When the pesticides are absorbed by birds and other animals, they move into the food chain, reducing fertility and causing other problems. Eventually, these pesticides may end up in humans, either through the food chain by ingestion or from direct contact with the treated food or fruit.

Satellite imagery now makes it possible to monitor large crops from the sky, detecting disease and insect problems before the human eye can see them. This early detection makes it possible to treat the limited problem area rather than the entire crop. It saves money, protects the harvest, and reduces the amount of pesticide used. The service is now cost effective and worthy of consideration for those in agriculture. Consideration of new developments such as this is especially appropriate for those who see the world as a gift from God to be used rather than exploited.

Recently, I became aware of a family who, one by one, became gravely ill. Mysteriously, the entire family was struck by frightening seizures, nausea, and emotional instability. They eventually traced their illness to pesticides used to treat their home for insects. In England, people are complaining that dogs are dying from the effects of pesticides sprayed on neighboring areas. We must also

> The kingdom of the world has become the kingdom of our Lord and of his Christ, and he will reign for ever and ever.
>
> Revelation 11:15

give careful thought to the kinds of chemicals we use to produce beautiful lawns, gardens, and insect-free homes. These chemicals may be dangerous to our children and us. Have you thought about the signs that companies are required to put up after spraying a lawn telling you it is dangerous to walk on the grass for twenty-four hours? A part of good stewardship is to be knowledgeable about what and how we use products to produce the effects we desire for beauty and comfort.

Fertilizers, when used appropriately, are actually quite marvelous. The way they can spur growth and create a healthy plant is impressive to anyone who has ever farmed or gardened. But fertilizers must also be used carefully. Too much fertilizer can burn plants or crops. The excess can also leach into the water system or drain into surrounding lakes and rivers, creating problems. Some lakes have literally died as a result of fertilizer draining into them over an extended period of time.

This discussion could apply to a number of related matters, such as the use of water for irrigation, but enough has been said to make the point that as Christians we need to be more thoughtful and concerned about how we use and treat the environment. God has given us the responsibility to preserve, enrich, and utilize his creation. As we grow spiritually, we should become more sensitive and discerning about such matters.

Underneath Are the Everlasting Arms

The benefit of God's sovereignty and the believer's responsibility for the use of power and authority is apparent. The greatness of God is of the greatest possible comfort and encouragement. God becomes the believer's security. Because God is in control, we may, with confidence, proceed to focus our attention on the productive side of subduing this world for his glory. Sidney Lanier conveyed this concept well in his famous poem "The Marshes of Glynn":

> As the marsh-hen secretly builds on the watery sod,
> Behold, I will build me a nest on the greatness of God:
> I will fly in the greatness of God as the marsh-hen flies
> In the freedom that fills all the space, twixt the marsh
>   and the skies:
> By so many roots as the marsh-grass sends in the sod
> I will heartily lay me a-hold on the greatness of God.[8]

Isaiah put it a different way, one equally useful. The creator of this world, mighty God that he is, does not get tired or grow weary (Isa. 40:28). If that is true, then no matter how impossible the dream, no matter how difficult the task, no matter how long it takes, the Lord is with us. That should inspire our best efforts.

Though some people may be overwhelmed by their circumstances and unable to continue, "Those who hope in the LORD will renew their strength. They will soar on wings like eagles; they will run and not grow weary, they will walk and not be faint" (Isa. 40:31). The Lord's grace will always be sufficient, regardless of what happens. This should provide whatever encouragement is needed so that you will be motivated to "give yourselves fully to the work of the Lord, because you know that your labor in the Lord is not in vain" (1 Cor. 15:58; see also 2 Cor. 12:9; Gal. 6:9).

Because God is sovereign and in control of this world, we also need not fear. This is important because fear paralyzes. It keeps us from acting or modifies our action from what it might have been. We learn to fear people early in life. We learn to fear evil and irresponsible people—the

> **We must remember throughout our lives that in God's sight there are no little people and no little places—only one thing is important: to be consecrated persons in God's place for us, at each moment. Those who think of themselves as little people in little places, if committed to Christ and living under his lordship in the whole of life, may, by God's grace, change the flow of our generation.**
>
> **Francis Schaeffer, *No Little People***

drunk driver, the angry person with a gun, the evil demagogue who doesn't care whom he destroys. We learn to fear strangers who may kidnap or rape. When our parents punished us, they not only taught us what was right, they taught us to fear what would happen if we did wrong.

Many people, therefore, are afraid to oppose evil because of what may happen to them if they do so. Some years ago, Kitty Genovese was murdered on the streets of a city. Thirty-eight people heard her scream for help while she was being stabbed to death. No one came to her defense. No one responded—not even to call the police. They were afraid to get involved.

The Christian learns not to fear people. Of course, we must use wisdom in dealing with potentially dangerous people, but ultimately we trust in God, knowing that he is sovereign. If we are right with the Lord and daily doing what he wants, we do not have to fear what others may do to us (Ps. 27:1–3; Rom. 8:31–39). We should not be overly concerned about adversaries or obstacles, for God is with us and for us. This fearless faith equipped earlier martyrs and inspires us today. Martin Luther had it right when he penned these now famous words, inspired by Psalm 46:

> A mighty fortress is our God,
> a bulwark never failing;
> our helper, he, amid the flood
> of mortal ills prevailing.
>
> The body they may kill,
> God's truth abideth still;
> his kingdom is forever.

The mature believer should be courageous in the face of evil forces or tyrants. When fear causes good people to fail to resist evil people or ideas, then such weakness allows bad people to gain strength and perhaps dominate. Such

---

We must not only serve God in our calling; our calling itself must be brought into alignment with God's Word.

Lee Hardy, *The Fabric of This World*

---

was the case in Germany. At one point Adolf Hitler might have been successfully resisted, but no one spoke up. The church, for the most part, was shamefully passive.

Just as the prophets spoke out against evil in their day, so should God's people speak out against and resist evil in our day (Eph. 5:11). This translates into a vocal, active citizenry who sees the necessity of political involvement. While on the one hand believers acknowledge that political solutions are not ultimate solutions and that winning elections is no assurance of a blessed future, they must support and vote for those people and causes that most clearly represent biblical values, remembering that being a devout Christian does not guarantee wise or just rule. They should also strive to remove people who prove evil or destructive, and they should oppose programs and causes that damage the common good. Failure to do so further empowers those who abuse the rights of others.

Finally, mature believers need not fear the future because they know it is in the Lord's hands. The unknown can be disturbing. It is often a cause of anxiety. Try as hard as we may to know the future, we cannot. Still, there is no reason to be afraid because we know God knows and controls the future. In addition, as believers we know that all things will work out for good for those of us who love God and trust in Christ (Rom. 8:28). We know that when we die we will go to be with God in heaven, where we shall experience indescribable bliss. At that time all the pain and sadness of this life with its disappointments and frustrations will be gone forever. We shall live forever with God and shall have new glorified bodies that are no longer subject to the limitations and frailty we now experience. One day this world, as we know it, shall be destroyed, and after the final judgment a new heaven and new earth shall be created for us to enjoy forever. "When we all get to heaven, what a day of rejoicing that will be."

To that we might add these words: "Then I heard a voice from heaven say, 'Write: Blessed are the dead who die in the Lord from now on.' 'Yes,' says the Spirit, 'they will rest from their labor, for their deeds will follow them'" (Rev. 14:13).

A Life of Purpose

God, through his sovereign power and providential care, is purposefully directing the flow of human history for his glory. In a similar manner, he expects believers to be guided by a clear purpose, or a stewardship of life. When we live according to such a purpose, we accomplish as much as we can with what we have during the time God gives us (Matt. 25:14–30).

Laziness and complacency are called into question when seen in the light of a stewardship of life for the glory of God. How can anyone be content merely to exist or survive when there are so many opportunities to serve the Lord? Life is too brief and our accountability too serious

> Every picture is more or less a character study of the one who painted it, just as generally the inner spiritual and moral human being expresses himself in every action.
>
> Caspar David Friedrich, *Caspar David Friedrich in Briefen and Bekenntnissen*

not to make the most of all our days. Though there are many acceptable activities and vocations, our responsibility is to discover the best stewardship of life.

Does that mean there is no time for play? Is it wrong to relax and take a break or enjoy a vacation? Must every working minute be filled with intense, productive activity? All we have to do is reflect on the Sabbath, the pattern of creation and the rhythm of life, to realize that we need time for mental and physical refreshment if we are to be our most productive. Work too many hours, become fatigued, and your productivity will suffer. Your decisions will not be as good. You may become irritable or more easily frustrated.

When you develop a sense of purpose, shaped by God's Word, then all your decisions and activities can be brought into alignment with it so that you can achieve maximum effectiveness with the time and resources God gives you. As you make decisions that will enable you to fulfill your God-given sense of purpose, you will reflect the character of God. That is your responsibility. Remember, it is not how long you live but how you live that counts. The day of reckoning awaits. Purposeful achievement is a mark of the sovereign rule of God coming to expression in your life.

QUESTIONS FOR REFLECTION

1. In what ways are you trying to be a good steward?
2. How should Christians best care for the creation? What priorities should we set?
3. What are your gifts and how are you using them in the area of stewardship?
4. How do power and influence fit into a biblical concept of stewardship?
5. What spheres of authority do you have? How do you use your authority?

CHAPTER SEVEN

THE
CREATOR GOD

IN THE BEGINNING GOD CREATED THE HEAVENS AND THE EARTH.

GENESIS 1:1

I n *The Idiot,* Prince Myskin is mocked for suggesting that
the world will be saved by beauty. His supposedly
ridiculous suggestion is attributed to the fact that he is
a Christian and has now fallen in love. As an object of
ridicule, he has no following or credence among those
who mock him. Then someone from the group suggests
that if Myskin had said the world will be saved by truth
or goodness, they would have understood. That would be
sensible. But to say the world will be saved by beauty—
only a fool would suggest that. Then someone asks, "What
if Prince Myskin, the holy fool, is right. What then?"

Similarly, when Christians talk of faith and spirituality,
they quickly think of holiness, truth, and love. Seldom do

the words *beauty* or *creativity* come to mind as characteristics of spiritual maturity. It has not always been so. St.
Augustine, for example, linked beauty to faith. Just as the
world and its beauty are inseparable and reveal the creator, so man bears the form or beauty of God since he is
created in his image. It becomes important, Augustine contends, for him to realize that God is both beautiful and
creator. So the psalmist said,

> One thing I ask of the LORD,
>   this is what I seek:
> that I may dwell in the house of the LORD
>   all the days of my life,
> to gaze upon the beauty of the LORD
>   and to seek him in his temple.
>
> Psalm 27:4

The creation of the universe not only attests to the
supreme omnipotence of God, it also displays his creativity in all its glory, for God is the author of beauty as well
as truth. In traveling the world, you cannot escape being
struck by its natural beauty. We sing of purple mountains'
majesty profiled against the beautiful blue spacious skies
that stretch from sea to shining sea. We capture its essence
in other ways as well: the gurgle of the cold, frothy, moun-
tain brook; the dramatic burst of yellow forsythia emerging from the drab bleakness of winter; the translucent
beauty of a rainbow perched in the sky; the magnificent
grandeur of a colossal waterfall; or the winter wonderland
created by a fresh snowfall. Add to that the graceful glide
of a deer through dappled woods, the proud strut of a
prairie partridge, or the cute antics of a playful, young
puppy. Then close your eyes and listen to the rhythmic
pounding of the surf or the whisper of the wind in the
palms. What a magnificent creation—the work of the quin-
tessential artist! No wonder Jesus said, "See how the lilies

of the field grow. They do not labor or spin. Yet I tell you that not even Solomon in all his splendor was dressed like one of these" (Matt. 6:28–29).

When God spoke the universe into reality out of nothingness, he did the unrepeatable. Try as we may, humans will never be able to do what he did. At the same time, however, as the Creator, he set a pattern for humans to do things that have never been done.

Creativity in History

When God made Adam and Eve in his image, he endowed them with a creative capacity in the sense of doing new and different things, innovating and discovering new possibilities in the world. He also gave them the ability to appreciate beauty wherever they found it and to reorder their world into new expressions of its natural beauty. They had the innate desire and capability to design and make things that would be beautiful and elevating to the human spirit.

The cultural mandate (Gen. 1:28) no doubt extended beyond organizing, directing, building, and producing to include aesthetic elements of harmony, color, sound, and so on. But the fall changed all of that, and Adam and Eve's experience of the beauty of the Garden was disrupted. They were banished to a world where thorns and thistles scratched and cut, where weeds choked out good plants, where tornadoes, volcanoes, and earthquakes destroyed the natural beauty of their world, which would be further ravaged by a great flood during the time of Noah. They realized things could never be the same again, but they did not realize how extensive the damage would eventually be.

Nonetheless, their creative impulse and ability came to expression in their descendants. It is interesting to note that in the line of Lamech, a descendant of Cain, there is a reference to the harp and flute as well as to implements of iron and bronze (Gen. 4:17–23). By the time of Solomon, a level of expertise and artistic expression had developed so far beyond that of the Genesis 4 period that the magnificent temple created during this time was an edifice of sophistication and refinement, known and spoken of every-

> **If we commit ourselves to saying that the Christian revelation discovers to us the nature of all truth, then it must discover to us the nature of the truth about Art among other things.**
> Dorothy Sayers, *Towards a Christian Aesthetic*

where in the ancient world. In Exodus we also read of Bezalel and Oholiab, skilled and creative craftsmen who became essential to the making of the tabernacle, the ark, all the furnishings, and the vestments of Aaron and his sons. The Lord told Moses he filled Bezalel with the Spirit of God and gave him his artistic skills. He also appointed Oholiab to help Bezalel complete this project, crafting objects of glory and beauty (Exod. 31:1–11; 35:30–36:2).

The giftedness of the human race, insofar as ability to create works of lasting beauty, is undeniable. The seven wonders of the ancient world are proof. Think about the enigmatic Sphinx keeping vigil before the great Pyramids, the verdant hanging gardens of Babylon or the temple of Artemis at Ephesus. Or consider the Athenian acropolis boasting the stately Parthenon, Erechtheum, and other buildings. In museums filled with artifacts, replicas, and reconstructions of the ancient period, you may examine the colorful paintings, the exquisite jewelry and ornamentation, and the architectural accomplishments of its artists and artisans. One's first experience in such museums can be overwhelming.

Through the sweep of human history we encounter much that dazzles us, a result of the ingenuity and artistry of various epochs. The carefully detailed and colorful patterns of oriental rugs, the sonorous beauty of the violin, the captivating canvases of the masters, and the sculpted statues of the Renaissance show that the artistic nature of God has left its imprint on the human soul. This legacy of music, art, and literature in all its rich variety has enriched our world immensely. To our delight, human creativity still flourishes.

The Consequences of the Fall

That aesthetic dimension of life, however, cannot hide the pain and suffering caused by sin, nor can it conceal completely the greed, pride, and perversion that has often accompanied it. Think, for example, of the thousands who slaved and died like animals to build the Pyramids, Sphinx, or Great Wall of China. They were little more than expendable fodder for their rulers. Cities and monuments to the human ego also bred their own problems. In addition to the cost of human capital and the tax on national treasuries, the cities themselves became the breeding grounds for disease and epidemics, which occasionally cost more lives than combat on the battlefield.

Art has historically been a powerful medium for revealing human struggles and suffering. Think of the pain and sorrow depicted in Vincent van Gogh's potato eaters. Take a step further with the art of Wassily Kandinsky. In the early part of the twentieth century, he blasted life's meaninglessness with accusations such as: "The strife of colours, the sense of the balance we have lost, tottering principles, unexpected assaults, great questions, apparently useless striving, storm and tempests, broken chains, oppositions and contradictions—these make up our harmony."[1]

Recent history is replete with examples of despair and a sense of meaninglessness coming to expression in the arts. H. R. Rookmaker, the well-regarded Dutch art historian, has ably pointed out the message of absurdity in the art of Pablo Picasso.[2] Evaluating the field of fine arts from the tumult and social upheaval of the 1960s, Rookmaker concluded that "art is dying as a high human endeavor. . . . But what has come into its place but anti-art, just as there is anti-philosophy, anti-theater and so on. It testifies to the fact that art is in a deep crisis at the same time that it is attracting so much attention."[3] Ingmar Bergman, after struggling with faith in God and then rejecting God's existence, eventually concluded that "on the whole . . . art is shameless, irresponsible . . . the movement is intense, almost feverish, like it seems to me, a snake-skin, full of ants. The snake itself has long been dead, eaten, deprived of its poison, but the skin moves, filled with meddlesome life."[4]

Unfeigned decadence is expressed in Andrès Serrano's presentation of a photograph of a crucifix encased in a vial of his urine. Items such as this have been sponsored by the National Endowment for the Arts, giving them a huge audience and credibility. The Brooklyn Museum of Art stirred a controversy in the fall of 1999 with some unusual displays including an exhibit featuring a portrait of the Virgin Mary daubed with elephant dung. Robert Mapplethorpe's erotic photographs are equally repugnant. Such presentations, by intention, are shockingly powerful statements, reminding us of sin's influence on human creativity.

Why has this happened to the arts? One answer is that art is usually tied to philosophy, to our understanding of ourselves, our world, and truth. It usually expresses the artist's understanding of life. In some instances, there is a conscious rejection of art and beauty as historically understood because of a different understanding of reality. As Gene Veith observes, "Today, works are often purposefully ugly. Their aim is not to give pleasure but to affront the sensibilities of their audience, thereby 'waking them up' to the meaninglessness of reality."[5]

So a stack of bricks or a piece of bent metal may be called art—as may a box of cat litter. You are probably familiar with many other "works of art" that attempt to convince the public of a more and more radical understanding of art. Veith explains this by asserting:

> Secularists today are genuinely unable to tell the difference between works with aesthetic merit and those with none. In this aesthetic vacuum, fashion statements, celebrity mongering, and political grantsmanship have come to dominate the art world. Art is lost. Those who would defend the arts must do so, ironically, against much of the contemporary artistic establishment, which seems bent on trivializing and vandalizing the rich legacy of human artistry. That this is done in the name of art only makes its hostility to aesthetic merit more perverse.[6]

The Gospel, Beauty, and Creativity

The gospel offers an escape from the deadening influence of sin that chokes the joy from life and dashes it to the ground, producing an ugly, broken mess. God converts the believer into a new person in Christ. As the Lord remakes that person in his image, he gives the believer a new ability to reshape life and the world into a thing of beauty reflective of God's own nature. The innovative, aesthetic dimensions of life find redemptive stimulation, and the corrosive, destructive tendency of sinful influence gradually diminishes as spiritual maturity increases. As the Bible states, "He has made everything beautiful in its time" (Eccles. 3:11). This is true of God's transforming influence on Christians. God's perfection is linked to his beauty, so as sin and its influence diminish, his beauty is manifested, though imperfectly, in us. God's creativity resulted in the making of not only new things but beautiful things. In similar fashion, as we become more like God, we become not only innovative or creative, but we develop a love for beauty and a desire to multiply it.

When you stop to think about it, some of the greatest literature, some of the most sublime music, the best art, and the grandest architecture have been produced by Christians. Though frequently cited for its failings, the church has contributed immensely to the enrichment and ennoblement of life by embracing and advocating beauty. What would civilization, especially Western civilization, be like without the influence of Christianity?

It is ironic, then, that Protestants since the Reformation have often been viewed as being opposed to art and beauty. Evangelicalism and fundamentalism in particular have not been noted for their encouragement of and contribution to various forms of art and culture. Rather, they have been

> **Our excuse for our esthetic failure has often been that we must be about the Lord's business, the assumption being that the Lord's business is never esthetic.**
>
> Clyde Kilby, *Christian Imagination*

perceived as engendering a suspicion of art's value. That criticism has frequently been justified. Not only is much evangelical religious music and art tacky, it often is merely an undiscerning copy of the world's music. Evangelicals to their detriment have often vigorously opposed popular culture in its diverse expressions, whether movies, TV, music, or dancing. Charles G. Finney, a famous evangelist of the nineteenth century, epitomized this attitude when he insisted, "I cannot believe that a person who has ever known the love of God can relish a secular novel."[7]

While the fine arts of classical music, literature, poetry, music, and theater eventually found some acceptance among believers, the pop or low-culture arts such as movies, television, and popular music continued to experience the same disapproval that Finney and other Christians directed toward "worldly amusements." Part of the difficulty, as William Romanowski has aptly noted, was that the clergy saw such entertainment as a threat to the values and practices that should be espoused by the church.[8] As the entertainment industry grew during the twentieth century, the church's adversarial approach cost it the opportunity for constructive interaction and an ameliorating influence. While some evangelical Christians correctly observed a relationship between entertainment and values, their response may not have been the most helpful. As Romanowski said,

> Instead of responding to the entertainment industry as to any other aspect of life that is corrupted by sin and in need of transformation, church leaders perceived it as part of a spiritual attack on Christian values and social institutions that imperiled not only the nation but also the Kingdom of God and righteous living.[9]

This mistake proved costly because it subsequently minimized Christian influence in these areas. Now mature believers must realize they have a responsibility to engage constructively in all aesthetic cultural expressions, supporting and encouraging those that are compatible with biblical principles. They also need to endeavor to transform those expressions that are incompatible, opposing them when appropriate.

As Christians, we are not only called to embrace cleanliness and righteousness, we are called to present the cleanliness attractively and to make the righteousness winsome and comely. Beauty, truth, and goodness must be permanent companions. Just as the loss of any one of the three distorts true Christianity, it also distorts all of life, including the arts.

Occasionally, Christians are led to believe that only art that is distinctly religious in subject matter is "real" Christian art. Anything else is not spiritual and does not fit a Christian context. This kind of thinking is as erroneous as Finney's condemnation of secular novels. Rookmaker's point is well taken.

> What is Christian in art does not lie in the theme, but in the spirit of it, in its wisdom and the understanding of the reality it reflects. Just as being a Christian does not mean going around singing hallelujah all day, but showing the renewal of one's life by Christ through true creativity, so a Christian painting is not one in which the figures have halos.[10]

These observations about creativity and beauty need not be restricted to the arts. They are equally pertinent to all of life, reminding us that our creativity and expressions of beauty should be incorporated into the fabric of daily life. The colors you use to paint your house, your choice of furniture and its placement contribute substantially to visual impact, comfort, and enjoyment. The psychological effect of these external factors is a reminder of how important they really are. As I drive home every day, my preferred route meanders along an interesting corridor of houses and buildings. It finally spills into an older residential area of varied but stately homes, canopied by magnificently majestic ancient oaks and cradled among the spring-fed lakes upon whose surfaces the evening sun dances. By the time I drive up to our home and park, I feel good. I never tire of that drive. Often, I think of how different it is for many other people.

Having built, bought, and lived in a number of homes through the years, I am well aware of the effort required to transform a house into an attractive haven. I am quite familiar with the importance of a neighborhood taking interest in its appearance as a whole, as well as each individual homeowner caring for his property. It is well worth the effort. Mature spirituality tries to achieve the conversion of one's environment into something as attractive as possible.

Paul's encouragement about embracing the lovely (Phil. 4:8) should be taken to heart by Christians. The mature believer who does so will work to make his or her environment better and more lovely than when first encountered and will continue to keep it attractive, perhaps even

> For as God is infinitely the greatest Being, so he is allowed to be infinitely the most beautiful and excellent; and all the beauty to be found throughout the whole creation, is but the reflection of the diffused beams of that Being . . . the foundation and fountain of all being and all beauty.
>
> Jonathan Edwards, *The Nature of True Virtue*

making improvements. Edward Bok is a good example. Near Lake Wales in Central Florida, he constructed a beautiful tower with a carillon and surrounded it with gardens. His purpose was to leave this world more beautiful than it was. He is, in this respect, an excellent model for other Christians.

The same case could be made for one's personal appearance. While it is easy to take such matters to extreme, there is good reason to suggest that it is entirely appropriate, actually obligatory, to pay attention to clothing, hair style, and personal hygiene as it affects one's appearance. Anne Hollander, in *Seeing through Clothes,* draws a relationship between art, the media, and clothing in the Western world, contending,

> When people put clothes on their bodies, they are primarily engaged in making pictures of themselves to suit their own eyes, out of the completed combination of clothing

152

and body. The people who do this most readily are those living in civilizations in which the naturalistic image of man is the cornerstone of art, and the pictures they make when they dress are directly connected to the pictures they ordinarily see and accept as real. Interesting changes in actual fashions of dress have coincided with the activity in representational art. In the nineteenth and twentieth centuries no less than in the fifteenth and sixteenth. . . . Visual fare must vary, and the looks of people are the staple of the visual diet.[11]

In talking about such matters, we tend to overlook philosophical connectedness. Stuart Ewen provides a superlative example by pointing out that the emergence of style as an important part of people's lives "cannot be separated from the evolution and sensibility of modernity." "Style," he notes, "is a visible reference point by which we have come to understand life in progress." He continues his argument: "On the one hand, style speaks for the rise of a democratic society, in which one who wishes to become is often seen as more consequential than who one is. On the other hand, style speaks for a society in which coherent meaning has fled to the hills, and in which drift has provided a context of continual discontent."[12]

While excessively opulent clothing may convey materialistic values incompatible with Christianity, a discerning eye for an affordable wardrobe enhances one's appearance and becomes an affirmation of beauty and grace. During the current era of chic grunge, believers would do well to be more thoughtful about a concern for beauty and truth than to mindlessly conform to secular trends and tastes that may conflict with that concern. Spirituality does come to expression in one's appearance.

Although this discussion has concentrated primarily on art and the relationship of the visual to beauty and creativity, similar analyses could be offered regarding music, theater, and film. In addition, although the connections are not always immediately recognized, beauty and creativity are equally relevant concerns in regard to church worship and architecture. We turn now to these topics.

Worship and Spirituality

In many Protestant churches, the sermon has been the focus; the rest of the service is peripheral. Elements of worship other than the sermon have received little or no attention or planning and have often been implemented perfunctorily. The result is an impoverished, hollow service that worshipers find unattractive and boring. This is inexcusable. Time and care need to be directed to the selection of music, the reading of Scripture, prayer, and confession—to the service as a whole. Today it is appropriate, if not necessary, to ask, Is the primary emphasis on the vertical dimension—worshiping God—or the horizontal—engaging the audience? How much of the worship service should be devoted to music? What music should be sung or played? What are the criteria for making these decisions? What will be the sequence of music and how will the music relate to the other parts of the service? Thirty years ago answering these questions would have been relatively easy because church worship services were fairly similar and traditional. That is no longer true. Today, battles are being fought over contemporary worship versus traditional worship.

George Truehart, addressing the current ferment in a provocative article in *The Atlantic Monthly*, predicts that worship will change dramatically in the future. How will the church be different? He is certainly not timid in suggesting a radical change.

No spires. No crosses. No robes. No clerical collars. No hard pews. No kneelers. No biblical gobbledygook. No prayerly

154

rote. No fire, no brimstone. No pipe organs. No dreary, eighteenth-century hymns. No forced solemnity. No Sunday finery. No collection plates. The list has asterisks and exceptions, but its meaning is clear. Centuries of European tradition and Christian habit are deliberately being abandoned, clearing the way for new, contemporary forms of worship and belonging.[13]

These developments and others like them are certainly not new, but they should cause us to reflect on the nature and ministry of the church. During the 1960s and 1970s, the church renewal movement flourished and many people expectedly reacted to things traditional. The renewal movement caused some evangelicals to consider the marks of the church. Francis Schaeffer entered into the discussion with his volumes *The Mark of the Christian* and *The Church before the Watching World.* He called for the practice of observable love, expressed by unity and community among believers, and the practice of the truth, expressed by orthodoxy of doctrine and purity of life. The evangelical community responded positively to his overture.

Centuries earlier, Martin Luther, John Calvin, and others of the Reformation era, in attempting to distinguish the true church from the false church, suggested characteristics that marked the true church. Consensus did not emerge immediately, but in time, three marks were identified: (1) the true preaching and teaching of the Word of God, (2) the proper administration of the sacraments, and (3) the right exercise of church discipline.

As was true during the Reformation, historical factors are sometimes such that we need to revisit the criteria that distinguishes the true church from the false church. Points of tension doctrinally and socially may dictate a need to clarify these criteria. In some present-day mainline denominations, the new marks of the church have to do with gender and sexual issues. In some large, trendsetting evan-

155

gelical churches, the new marks of the church have to do with music and worship. For example, Truehart says, "Music, more than any other issue or symbol . . . divides congregations on the cusp of growth."[14]

Given the ferment, especially among evangelical churches, perhaps we need a fresh, informed discussion of the marks of a true church. Worship may be one of those key issues. Unless this matter receives careful attention, the present uncoupling could easily lead to aberration or worse.

Undoubtedly, how we worship cannot be separated from our understanding of God and our theology. Can the spiritually mature person worship God without giving careful consideration to these matters? The answer should be plain. Ignoring such concerns points to a serious deficiency.

In addition to having a worship service that is planned as a unified whole, coheres, and moves toward accomplishing its purpose, we must consider the context. What

> **The Christian is the one whose imagination should fly beyond the stars.**
>
> Francis Schaeffer, *Art and the Bible*

about the appearance of the building inside and out? What about the relationship of the building to its environment? What about the use of space, arrangement of seating, colors of fabric, walls, and ceiling? What about the lighting? Is it adequate? Does it support other contextual elements?

I raise some of these questions because usually too little thought is given to them. We have a tendency to keep doing the same things in the same ways or mindlessly copying something new and popular. We often perpetuate architectural models without giving thought to beauty and function. As a result, we sometimes have attractive buildings that do not serve the intended purpose. Sometimes the buildings are ugly monstrosities, monuments to an architect's imagination and ego.

If space, color, and similar factors are so important to interior design, and if aesthetics, ambiance, and so on are so important to a dinner party, why should these things be ignored when the Lord's people gather to worship? Our neglect of such matters must be a tacit declaration that, in our opinion, they are irrelevant. Granted, we are called to worship the Lord in the beauty of holiness, not the holiness of beauty (1 Chron. 16:29; Ps. 29:2). Nonetheless, beauty is an important factor, and it is equally wrong to ignore this aspect of worship. As Pierre Babin has convincingly written in *The New Era in Religious Communication,* these factors do matter.[15] Form and content should find an appropriate unity, a harmonious unity. Expressions of beauty must fit a particular culture and period in history. When these converge, the result is a powerful statement.

From Beauty to Creativity

Being remade in the image of God also moves us beyond an embrace and advocacy of beauty to an affinity with innovation, inventiveness, and newness. While a wide range of giftedness affects our potential expressions of creativity, as those who are growing spiritually to become more like the creator, we should embrace creativity as it is used in positive and beneficial ways.

We must remember there can be a dark side to this creative aspect of our nature. Just as unbelievers may think up new and more terrible ways to torture, or exploit others for their own purposes, or steal through counterfeit production or Internet scams, so the Lord's people should think of new ways to counter evil and improve circumstances for all people. We should think of new ways to eliminate pollution, improve prosthetics, or build houses. Remembering the power of evil to seduce, we should be spiritually motivated to come up with better ideas and more winsome alternatives. Our redeemed creativity should express itself in this way just as it should through positive expression in the arts.

Most of us utilize an infinitesimal percentage of our brain's potential, so we are told. Explanations of this matter are not effusively offered, but the effects of sin make the most sense to me because sin restricts and destroys. If that is so, then spiritual growth should spur us to appreciate the potential granted by the Lord and to use more of that mental potential for his glory. Since a typical educational experience breeds conformity, the imagination and native curiosity with which we are born are gradually strangled. Therefore, we need to stimulate the imagination and encourage curious, persistent investigation of various components of life. For the moment, such activities may appear to be a waste of time, but they may lead to new and better ways of understanding ourselves and the world. Drama, art, music, and literature are a few means of providing that stimulation. Curiosity, tinkering, exploring, and other forms of investigative activity are other equally valid forms of stimulation.

The cultivation of quiet time, down time, and holiday time may be a step in that direction as well. Typically, almost every minute of our day is filled with activity, even if nothing more than watching television. There is always something to do. If not, we find something to do. Sound pursues us doggedly into every nook and cranny of life because we abhor the sound of silence. When we do this to ourselves, the creative juices are stilled. So make some time for yourself to be alone, quiet, and contemplative—

hard as it may be at first—and you will be surprised to see a new aspect of yourself emerging.

The Lord decreed a Sabbath so that in spite of the heavy demands of life we could have time to refresh body and spirit. As we recognize his divine provision and begin to use it as he intended, we find the refreshment that is needed, not only to assure maximum productivity in our work but also to allow stimulation of mind and spirit. As we have time to reflect, inquire, assimilate, and experience that deep satisfying rush as creative juices begin to surge within us, we sense new vistas of exploration and understanding.

Another way in which creativity may come to expression is through procreation. Giving birth to children who bear your likeness as well as the Lord's is a wonderfully creative experience. The nurture of those children into adults, shaping their thought and behavior, is not only a solemn responsibility but a marvelous adventure as you play a role in shaping something beautiful and a lasting force for good. Do it poorly, however, and the final result may be destructive for both your family and society.

The issue of quality and craftsmanship adds another dimension to this discussion. When high quality work is produced by Christians who are concerned to demonstrate the integrity of their expertise and their faith, it may

> The intuitive powers of the imagination can leap beyond the sometimes leaden abstractions with which reason must work . . . to assimilate the data of the world into a deeper vision of faith.
>
> Gregory Wolfe, *The New Religious Humanism*

become compellingly influential. Recently, our school constructed a new building. Quite a bit of thought and interaction by our faculty, staff, students, and board helped shape the building that was finally constructed. It is well built, attractive, and functional. An alumnus who is a fine craftsman finished the conference rooms and administrative offices with hand milled solid walnut paneling and moldings. It is unusual and quite striking. Almost everyone who visits is favorably impressed. There is no doubt that it has given these rooms a distinctive beauty. I can't help but conclude that this concern for quality and attractiveness should be typical of all Christians as they seek to reflect the creative character of God.

Christians should also be concerned about developing a new body of art for succeeding generations. The media of music, film, and visual arts are especially powerful because they often have a shaping influence beyond the written or spoken word. Consider, for instance, the popularity of music among today's teens, who have been referred to as a vibration generation. Christians who bring

> Art . . . is cognitive; it discovers and knows and tells, tells the reader how things are, how we are, in a way that the reader can confirm with as much certitude as a scientist taking a pointer-reading.
>
> Walker Percy, quoted in *The New Religious Humanism*

their understandings of faith and life to fuller experience through these media create platforms for significant influence. Rather than condemning these media, Christians should look for ways to get involved, develop expertise, and produce material that is good, true, and beautiful. It can be done, and there is no good reason why Christians should not embrace all the arts and encourage a level of participation that can make a positive difference. A bracing introduction to recent and current developments in the relationship of Christianity to culture, especially literature, is found in *The New Religious Humanism*, particularly the chapter titled "The Christian Writer in a Fragmented Culture."[16]

At the same time new materials are being developed, it is certainly appropriate to stimulate a renewed interest in good literature, music, drama, and art that is already available. Recently, while in London, I was able to attend J. B. Priestly's play *An Inspector Calls*. It was as powerful a statement about compassion and justice as any sermon I have heard. So much marvelous material is already a part of our heritage, and it would be a tragic loss to ignore it.

At the very least, spiritually mature Christians should have enough discernment to avoid ersatz beauty. They should not help fuel the popularity of the tawdry or ugly. The violence and promiscuity of movies and the dissonance of heavy metal music are in a similar category. It is better to advocate and support constructive alternatives more in harmony with biblical principles. If the public can't find satisfactory alternatives, it may be because of our failure to provide them. If we have not seized the moment to produce what could capture the imagination of believers and unbelievers and shape a better tomorrow, then we have no one to blame but ourselves.

Finally, we realize that even if we enrich and adorn ourselves and our world with our embrace of beauty and creativity and if we innovate and invent, this world shall always bear the ugly scar of sin. Therefore, our inner insatiable hunger for the beautiful leads us to appreciate the insight of C. S. Lewis all the more:

> In one way, of course, God has given us the morning star already. You can go and enjoy the gift on many fine mornings if you get up early enough. What more, you may ask, do we want? Ah, but we want so much more—something the books on aesthetics take little notice of. But the poets and the mythologies know all about it. We do not want merely to see beauty, though, God knows, even that is

bounty enough. We want something else which can hardly be put into words—to be united with the beauty we see, to pass into it, to receive it into ourselves, to bathe in it, to become a part of it. That is why we have peopled air and earth and nature with gods and goddesses and nymphs and elves—that though we cannot, yet these projections can enjoy in themselves that beauty, grace and power of which Nature is the image. That is why the poets tell us such lovely falsehoods. They talk as if the west wind could really sweep into a human soul; but it can't. They tell us that "beauty born of a murmuring sound" will pass into a human face; but it won't. Or not yet. For if we take the imagery of Scripture seriously, if we believe that God will one day give us the Morning Star and cause us to put on the splendor of the sun, then we may surmise that both the ancient myths and the modern poetry, so false as history, may be very near the truth as prophecy. At present we are on the outside of the world, the wrong side of the door. We discern the freshness and purity of morning, but they do not make us fresh and pure. We cannot mingle with the splendors we see. But all the leaves of the New Testament are rustling with the rumor that it will not always be so. Some day, God willing, we shall get in. . . . And in there, in beyond Nature, we shall eat of the tree of life.[17]

As we look forward to that great day to which C. S. Lewis pointed, our anticipation of it will motivate us with greater love for the Lord because he makes it possible. It will also push us to be more like our great Creator, who will bring us to the splendor of a new heaven and a new earth. As we grow spiritually and reflect God's creative character more and more, we will cultivate creativity, whether by being creative or embracing the creativity of others, and pursue beauty, whether by our own efforts or the recognition and use of the aesthetic contributions of others. So shall our lives and the world become more lovely to those around us.

QUESTIONS FOR REFLECTION

1. Is there a relationship between beauty and morality?
2. How important is the aesthetic dimension of life?
3. How do you evaluate movies, music, art, and literature in the light of Scripture?
4. Have Christians been more helpful or more harmful in an aesthetic improvement of life during the last one hundred years? Why?

CHAPTER EIGHT

INCH BY INCH

LIKE NEWBORN BABIES, CRAVE PURE SPIRITUAL MILK, SO THAT
BY IT YOU MAY GROW UP IN YOUR SALVATION, NOW THAT YOU
HAVE TASTED THAT THE LORD IS GOOD.

1 PETER 2:2

In the Bible, spiritual growth is compared to human growth and development (Eph. 4:13–16; Heb. 5:12; 1 Peter 2:2; 2 Peter 3:18), and rightly so, because they are similar. Since we are familiar with physical aging from our daily experience, we can easily visualize spiritual growth as a process of change. Even though spiritual growth is essentially inward and invisible, and therefore, more difficult to observe, there are external expressions and telltale indicators of growth, as we noted earlier.

Birth is an exciting, happy time—a cause for celebration. To think that the arrival of a tiny, squalling, wrinkled infant could be the source of such overwhelming emotions is remarkable. It is paralleled by the joy shared when someone becomes a Christian. Not only does the new believer experience joy, but so do those Christians who were involved in his or her conversion. Great joy and celebration take place in heaven too (Luke 15:7).

Birth is an entrance into life, and it becomes an invitation to lifelong growth. The same is true of spiritual birth, or being born again. An acceptance of Christ as Lord and Savior opens the door to eternal life, and it also marks the beginning of a lifelong process of spiritual growth. Other

> Superficiality is the curse of our age. The doctrine of instant satisfaction is a primary spiritual problem. The desperate need today is not for a greater number of intelligent people, or gifted people, but for deep people.
>
> Richard Foster, *Celebration of Discipline*

parallels also exist, such as dependence. Newborn babies cannot care for themselves. Without constant care and feeding, they cannot survive. In the ancient world, parents who did not want their baby because it was the wrong sex or for other reasons put it outside to fend for itself. Soon after abandonment and without care, the baby died. People who experience a new spiritual birth are spiritually dependent, weak, and ignorant, like infants. If God withdrew or abandoned them, they would be doomed because they are dependent on him. They are also dependent on other Christians for direction and encouragement.

Babies know very little at birth. They must learn to communicate by learning syllables, then words, and finally sentences. They face the challenge of learning to eat, first, greedily sucking milk, then swallowing spoonfuls of mushy baby food, and finally feeding themselves solid food with a spoon and fork. The newborn Christian listens to sermons, reads the Bible, and begins to learn. In due time, the searching mind will seek to understand deeper concepts and thoughts, but first, basic information is needed. Once a foundation has been laid, matters of complexity and difficulty may be explored.

Although basic patterns and time thresholds are associated with human growth and development, there is also a great deal of diversity. It is fascinating—at times frustrating—to note the extent of that diversity among our own children. They may grow at different rates with spurts at varied ages. They develop different interests.

So it is with spiritual growth. Substantial variety exists among believers in their spiritual development. Some people exhibit purity but have trouble loving their fellow Christians. Others have a strong sense of stewardship but no obedience. I know a woman who has a huge capacity for love,

> The keeping and right managing of the heart in every condition is the great business of a Christian's life.
>
> John Flavel, *A Saint Indeed*

but she seems to lack wisdom. Her deficiency in wisdom affects the way she lavishly reaches out to others in love. If her love were tempered by wisdom, would she more consistently and carefully discipline her children? Is she too accepting of people who manipulate and use her? Does her love create a positive or negative effect? Giftedness may lead to more rapid development in certain areas of the spiritual life, but these areas need to be balanced by growth in other areas as well. The more we grow to reflect all the attributes of God, the more beneficial our spiritual growth will be and the more it will reflect the true character of God. Though we are all different, with different gifts and personalities, our spiritual quest calls us to broad, balanced growth.

A Time-Consuming Process

Physical development is a slow process. So is spiritual growth. Though spurts of physical growth may occur now and then, growth is usually so slow that it is almost imperceptible from day to day. When you look in the mirror every day, you see essentially the same person you saw the last time you looked. You do not notice distinctive changes. But you are changing more than you may realize! When you nostalgically flip though an old photograph album or encounter a picture from years past, you are suddenly struck by how much you have changed. You think, *I used to look like that! What a difference now!* The same is true of your parents or your children. We are all aging day by day, and though the change is imperceptible, as you review longer spans of time, you are confronted with the reality of that change.

Typically, spiritual growth also occurs steadily and unobtrusively. It is a part of the daily flow of your life, so that while you are conscious of certain experiences and their influence, you do not normally think of them in the context of your overall spiritual growth. When you consider an overview of your life pilgrimage, however, you can often see evidence of change and growth in your spiritual life, just as photos reveal physical change and growth.

For a generation always in a hurry, used to instant results, and demanding speed at all costs, slow growth is a misfit. When people want quick, sure solutions and ten swift steps to success, the Lord's deliberate pace is frustrating. Where can we find an inclination toward the long term or the patient attitude that should accompany it? Even when we acknowledge the need to be patient and the reality of the distance run, we are still faced with the cultural pressure and mind-set: "Do it now, get it over with, and move on to the next thing." We must realize we will never achieve perfection this side of heaven, and we must expect our spiritual development to be a life-long process. It should bring us nearer to the goal of conformity to the image of God, but there will always be another step. So we must commit ourselves to think long term, to persevere.

There are no shortcuts to human development. Try to push a young child to ride a bike too soon and the usual result is that it happens later rather than sooner. Attempts to find or make shortcuts to spiritual growth are also counterproductive. This is probably why Paul warned the church not to ordain new believers. When people are thrust too quickly into leadership responsibilities before they are ready, they can experience setbacks or lose their motivation to grow. I recall someone who became a church officer after being a Christian only a short time. He was talented

> Until having at length finished our course, we work the good which thou has set before us, that having at last gone through all the evils of this life, we may come to that blessed rest which has been prepared for us in heaven by Christ our Lord.
>
> John Calvin, *Devotions and Prayers of John Calvin*

and a successful businessman, but he was spiritually immature. When he found himself in the midst of a turbulent church problem, he did not respond with spiritual prudence. As a result, the church suffered severe damage to relationships that could have been avoided with mature leadership. Rather than becoming an opportunity for growth, this experience caused him to become cynical about the church and reduced his motivation to grow.

Slow, seemingly imperceptible growth is not only frustrating to a quick fix world, it can also be discouraging. Like walking in a desert or swimming in an ocean, after hours of exertion, when no end is in sight, you become quite discouraged. You wonder if you will ever make it;

you wonder if it is really worth the effort. That is the point at which discouragement strikes.

Florence Chadwick, the first woman to swim the English Channel in both directions, attempted to become the first woman to swim from Catalina Island to the California coast. The water was numbing cold, and the fog was so thick she could hardly see the boats accompanying her. Millions watched on national television that Fourth of July in 1952 as the hours ticked slowly away. Suspense built as on several occasions sharks swimming alarmingly close had to be driven away with rifles. On she swam—resolutely. Fatigue was not a problem but the bone-chilling, frigid water was.

After being in the water for fifteen hours and fifty-five minutes, Florence quit, only to discover she was quite close to shore—only a half mile away. A dense fog had kept her from realizing how close she had come to her goal. Later she said, "If I had only been able to see the coast I would have made it." It was the only time she ever quit. Later she tried again and was successful, but her experience that day is instructive.

When you have no sense of progress and no clear understanding of where your goal is or how much effort or time it will take to reach it, you can lose motivation. The reason is clear: You cannot be sure you will make it, or you may not even be sure you are headed in the right direction. Perhaps you have lost sight of the goal. So you quit. This may explain the dismal failure of so many Christians to lead changed lives. Unsure of the goal or how to measure progress, they quit trying.

Though progress is slow, there are usually milestones along the way to remind you where you once were at various stages in the spiritual journey. It is imperative to look back and remind yourself of those milestones and the very real progress you have made. Such a reminder and a fresh vision of the celestial city may be enough to pull you, the modern "pilgrim," from the "Slough of Despond" and set you on your way again with a clear eye and a brisk step.

Growth as an Ordeal

In both spiritual development and physical development, the reality of adversity is apparent. Disease and illness are always a danger, and we never know when accidents or injuries will occur. As we grow and learn, we

> The Gospel of Jesus Christ is nothing if not a gospel of growth. It sets our eyes on a development more complete than any that can be conceived by a psychology confined within the limits of nature.
>
> Paul Tournier, *A Place for You*

inevitably make mistakes. Some are more painful to us; some are more painful to others. We can easily note the spiritual parallels. Consider the spiritual illnesses that can weaken us or the injuries that can harm us. You become severely depressed following the loss of an important job. Your child dies within the first year. Your parents reject you because you have become a Christian.

The path of perseverance for the spiritual pilgrim is treacherous. It is frought with danger, and challenges threaten at every turn. How we wish it could be compared to a pleasant walk in a garden on a beautiful, crisp, spring day. Though there are such memorable moments, they seem to occur so seldom. As Scott Peck has sagely observed, "Life is difficult."[1]

Life is a struggle. We progress and grow. Gains and improvements come, but often at a cost. Conflict and hardship cannot be evaded. No pain, no gain seems to be true for the Christian life as well as for sports. This axiom seems to be the point of the author of Hebrews, who, writing to those who would suffer, pointed to the example of believers who suffered in the past (Heb. 11:1–39). This served as a motivation for them to have a positive attitude toward their own suffering and to see the spiritual benefits rather than become discouraged (Heb. 12:3–5). Acknowledging that hardship is not pleasant, he reminds the reader, "Later on, however, it produces a harvest of righteousness and peace for those who have been trained by it" (Heb. 12:11).

Jesus' life is another source of encouragement when we face spiritual hardships. He moved through the various stages of childhood and youth, finally launching his ministry during early adulthood. Though his ministry was brief, it was painful. Not only was he opposed by religious leaders and other authorities, he ultimately faced death, accepting the judgment of God against sin for our sake. It is understandable that he prayed for the cup to pass so that he would not have to drink its judgment, yet Jesus was determined to do the will of the Father. The agony of his prayerful struggle testified to the intense ordeal of preparation he endured (Luke 22:44). Then he was tortured and crucified.

He had to endure such hardship in order to rise again and ascend triumphantly to the right hand of the Father, where he now sits with all authority and power. Because

> God is more concerned about our character than our comfort. His goal is not to pamper us physically but to perfect us spiritually.
>
> Paul W. Powell

he endured the conflict and emerged victoriously on the other side, we know that he is a sympathetic listener when we come to him in times of difficulty (Heb. 4:14–16). He understands. Our Lord will not forget us during our struggles. Though others may abandon us during a crisis, he never will. He will help us and enable us to make it to the other side to be with him.

With this in mind, Peter encouraged believers who were suffering "grief in all kinds of trials" to persevere, because he knew that it was a refining process during which their faith would be proved genuine and strong (1 Peter 1:6–7; 4:12–19). All believers should find the same encouragement during life's pain and hardships. Though encouragement doesn't diminish the pain, it makes the pain easier to endure. The ability to endure—perseverance—is decisive regarding your realization of spiritual maturity

Sufferings and hardships also make us more aware that we are dependent on the Lord. We do not have enough stamina and willpower to make it through life on our own. We need help. And when we admit our weakness and vulnerability, we discover his strength. The Lord's grace is always sufficient, as Paul observed when reflecting on his persecutions and his struggles with a thorn in the flesh (2 Cor. 11:23–12:10).

Stimulants and Impediments

It is difficult to ignore the fact that external conditions are a vital factor regarding growth and development. Children need nutritious food, a loving family, the proper health care, and a good education to grow and develop. As we get older, a healthy lifestyle and supportive relationships become more important.

Spiritual growth also requires positive stimulation and the proper "nutrition." The means of grace described in chapter 2—the Word, prayer, and the sacraments—therefore, are essential to growth. If you are a believer and genuinely desire spiritual growth that will please God and draw you closer to him, then it would be beneficial for you to pursue earnestly these means of grace. Spiritual growth does not usually occur apart from regular participation in these activities.

Regarding God's Word, attempt to read your Bible regularly, listening to its meaning with your heart as well as
with your mind. You may want to try one of the available
plans for reading through the Bible in a year, or you may
prefer to develop your own plan. Either way, let the Bible's
message suffuse your consciousness and penetrate your
thought. Study the Word of God seriously and diligently.
This may be done privately with the help of commentaries,
Bible dictionaries, and a good study Bible, or it may be
pursued in Bible study groups and through careful attention to the explanation of Scripture in sermons. There is
no satisfactory substitute, however, for reading and studying the Bible yourself so that you will clearly understand
its unified message and God can write its meaning and
implications on your heart.

As an earnest believer, you also need to pray to the Lord
regularly, asking his help and guidance so that you will be
strong and wise in serving him. The Bible states that you
should not expect to receive if you do not ask for his help
(Matt. 7:7–8). As an expression of complete dependence
on him for his provision and protection, prayer strength-
ens the bond between you and the Lord. Although the Lord

> When we speak of a man's walk and conversation, we mean his
> habits, the constant tenor of his life. . . . Persevere in the same
> way in which you have begun.
>
> **Charles Spurgeon,** *Morning and Evening*

does not promise to respond to your requests by granting
exactly what you ask, you may be assured that his love will
motivate him to give what is good for you (Matt. 7:7–11).
A life without prayer will doubtlessly be a barren one spiritually, so the sincere believer will look for opportunities
to communicate with God through prayer. Indeed, such a
person will experience an earnest desire to learn to pray

more effectively, perhaps with a prayer partner or mentor. Books of written prayers can also serve as helpful guides.

Another means of grace is participation in the ministry and worship of a local congregation, including the sacraments. Active involvement in a vibrant community of faith should lead to a deepening and strengthening of your faith as you add your voice to others in worshiping the Lord. Join with them gladly in ministry to one another and to the world. The example and encouragement of other believers is a powerful influence as you seek to grow spiritually and serve God. Engagement in the regular activities and ministry of a congregation not only gives expression to your faith but provides an opportunity to use your gifts to benefit others, whether through teaching, evangelizing, organizing, or serving in other capacities. Through your ministry involvement, you will be strengthened far more than those who remain passive observers. That is undoubtedly why the author of Hebrews urged, "Let us not give up meeting together, as some are in the habit of doing, but let us encourage one another—and all the more as you see the Day approaching" (Heb. 10:25). Withdraw and atrophy. Engage and develop.

Participation in the worship and life of a congregation includes the two sacraments, baptism and the Lord's Supper. As you join regularly with a congregation in observing these sacramental symbols of our salvation, you will be strengthened spiritually. Baptism enables you to affirm your cleansing from sin and union with God through

> We do not quit when we find that we are not yet mature and that there is a long journey still before us.
>
> **Eugene Peterson**, *A Long Obedience in the Same Direction*

Christ's atonement. The Lord's Supper is a vivid reminder of his death on the cross in order to suffer the punishment for our sins. It portrays God's acceptance of you, unworthy as you are, as well as his continuing nurture of you spiritually and your fellowship with other believers with whom you are one in Christ. The presence and grace of God experienced during such moments deepens your commitment and draws you closer to the Lord.

It should be apparent from what has been said so far that the means of grace are vital to the spiritual welfare of a believer and should not be neglected. Therefore, they are appropriately emphasized and encouraged as a necessity to Christian living and spiritual growth. But they are not to be confused with the characteristics of spiritual maturity. They are the vehicles to help you reach maturity but are not to be equated with it.

Emphasizing the positives does not reduce the need to minimize negative influences. Just as we learn that smoking is harmful to our health and that drugs can destroy our minds and lives, so we need to learn what negative influences can stunt our spiritual growth. Passion, the allure of sexual gratification, is inflamed by exposure to pornography, so it should be avoided. Greed can gobble up good intentions, so avoid placing yourself in the way of temptation to steal. Control the amount of time you spend watching television as well as what you watch on television. It is difficult to argue that too much TV or the wrong kinds of programs are beneficial to spiritual growth. Don't let TV make an addict of you. When you know a person or people may have a bad influence on you, avoid them. Just as your children need to stay out of gangs and away from drug dealers, so you must avoid people who can lead you astray.

Perhaps you are too busy. You may be the kind of person who never says no to any opportunity. Perhaps you have become a workaholic. If so, you may find yourself becoming hollow inside. Concentration slips. Productivity slides too. Creative juices dry up. Now is the time to take a break and find a way to ease off. Allow time for the Lord to speak and for you to become more reflective and intentional about what you are doing. Scheduling several breaks yearly to go away to pray, meditate, and listen to God may be beneficial.

Money, sex, and power have an appeal that can consume. Yet at the end of life, they can leave you empty and disillusioned, for in and of themselves they cannot satisfy. Do not misunderstand me. I am not saying that money, sex, and power are evil; each has its place, and a useful one. Nor am I saying you should not work hard and strive to

> Just as God led the people of Israel out of captivity in Egypt into the Promised Land, so the Christian life can be seen as a slow process of deliverance from bondage to sin before being let triumphantly into the heavenly city.
>
> Alister McGrath, *Christian Spirituality*

achieve. However, it is undeniable that some people, some things, and some situations have a corrosive influence, eating away at your soul, destroying your spiritual motivation, and eventually bringing you into bondage to them. Like diseases, they cause spiritual sickness. Avoid these things—whatever they may be. Do not be tempted by their appeal. Remember what they will do to you. Do you really want to end up spiritually dwarfed and defeated?

The Need for Giants

This is not a new problem. The complaint from the author of Hebrews is that many spiritual infants who should have grown up with the passage of time and assumed the responsibilities of adulthood had instead remained infants, continuing to require the time and energy that should have been directed toward others (Heb. 5:11–14). The same can be said today. Because some believers have not progressed as expected, they have become a burden on the believing community and deprived the church of the mature strength and leadership it needs to fulfill its mission.

We need spiritual giants desperately. We need them now. There is always a clamor for leaders, especially in trying times like ours that are dominated by a secular spirit. We need Christians of character, dignity, and wisdom who can stand tall against the spirit of our age. But we will not have them until we become serious about the process of spiritual growth and commit ourselves to persevere through all life's difficulties, running the race with patience so that we may become strong in the Lord.

It is possible to apply this same concept of growth and development to a culture or civilization. Although there are periods of dramatic change insofar as revival or renewal are concerned, change in a culture is also a process. Christianity did not lose its influence suddenly; it happened

> Each morning is a new beginning of our life.
> Dietrich Bonhoeffer, *Meditating on the Word*

over a period of years. Spiritual power and influence will not reappear suddenly either. But a faith commitment, with dogged perseverance, that leads us through the stages of spiritual growth may produce a new generation crowned with the glory of his grace, bearing his characteristics, leading his people into a future of hope and goodness. If this is to happen, the Christian community must develop a mind-set for the long run, doing what needs to be done and doing it well with patience and charity. Mature believers will understand this and lead the way in helping God's people as a community work toward this goal rather than hoping for a quick fix. In time, if we persevere, we shall overcome!

Remember the words of Bilbo Baggins, in J. R. R. Tolkien's *The Fellowship of the Ring,* as he left the shire on his 111th birthday:

> The Road goes ever on and on
> Down from the door where it began.
> Now far ahead the Road has gone,
> And I must follow, if I can,
> Pursuing it with eager feet,
> Until it joins some larger way
> Where many paths and errands meet
> And whither then? I cannot say.[2]

So, pilgrim, follow the road to spiritual maturity, patiently, diligently, and determinedly. And, happily, you know where the road ends.

QUESTIONS FOR REFLECTION

1. Draw a graph of your spiritual growth since conversion. Make your conversion the starting point and today the stopping point. Draw a horizontal line between the two, representing what you consider average in your spiritual development. List activities, events, difficulties, and victories by placing a dot to signify where they occurred in the time line of your life. The dots below the line represent periods of spiritual immaturity and periods of regression. Those above the line represent progress toward spiritual maturity that is above average. Why does your graph look the way it does? What would you most like to change?

2. What events and people have most helped you grow spiritually?
3. List the major impediments to your spiritual growth. What should you do about them?
4. What person would you choose as your spiritual mentor if you could choose anyone? Why?
5. What will you do as a result of reading this book?

NOTES

CHAPTER 1

1. St. Augustine, *Confessions,* trans. Henry Chadwick (Oxford: Oxford University Press, 2000), 3.

2. George Gallup Jr. and Timothy Jones, *The Next American Spirituality* (Colorado Springs: Chariot Victor, 2000).

3. Harvey Cox, *Fire from Heaven* (Reading, Mass.: Addison Wesley, 1995), xv–xvi.

4. *Newsweek,* 28 November 1994, 55.

5. Cynthia Barnett, *Software Metaphysician Florida Trend,* September 1999.

6. William D. Hendricks, *Exit Interviews* (Chicago: Moody Press, 1993), 258ff.

7. Robert Wuthnow, *After Heaven: Spirituality in America Since the 1950's* (Los Angeles: University of California Press, 1998), 2.

8. Richard Lovelace, *The Dynamics of Spiritual Life* (Downers Grove, Ill.: InterVarsity Press, 1979), 11–12.

9. *Christianity Today,* 5 April 1996, 29.

10. Ibid., 33.

11. *Christianity Today,* 5 February 1996, 29.

12. Ibid., 30. See also Richard J. Foster, *Celebration of Discipline,* rev. ed. (New York: HarperSanFrancisco, 1988).

13. Ibid., 29.

14. Wuthnow, *After Heaven,* 198.

CHAPTER 2

1. John Calvin, *Institutes of the Christian Religion,* ed. John T. McNeill, trans. Ford Lewis Battles (Philadelphia: Westminster Press, 1977), 40–41.

2. Ford Lewis Battles, ed., *The Piety of John Calvin* (Grand Rapids: Baker, 1978), 13. For further illustrations see Harold Begbie, *Twice-Born Men* (New York: Revell, 1909).

3. Susan Bergman, *Martyrs* (San Francisco: HarperSanFrancisco, 1996).

CHAPTER 3

1. John Naisbitt, *Megatrends* (New York: Warner Books, 1982), 39.

2. Francis Schaeffer, *True Spirituality* (Wheaton: Tyndale House, 1971), i.

3. Francis Schaeffer, *The Church before the Watching World* (Downers Grove, Ill.: InterVarsity Press, 1971), 79.

4. Henri Nouwen, *The Living Reminder* (San Francisco: Harper & Row, 1976), 31.

5. Kallistos Ware, "The Human Person as an Icon of the Trinity," *Sobermost* 8, (1986): 20, quoted in Craig Gay, *The Way of the (Modern) World* (Grand Rapids: Eerdmans, 1999), 294.

6. If you are interested in pursuing the manifestations of God's love in your life, you may also want to explore the "one another" passages in the Bible, for they give additional insight into the benefits and obligations of human relationships. You will find them readily in a concordance.

CHAPTER 4

1. Leon Uris, *Armageddon* (New York: Doubleday, 1962), 193.

2. Allan Bloom, *The Closing of the American Mind* (New York: Simon and Schuster, 1987), 25.

3. J. I. Packer, *Keep in Step with the Spirit* (Old Tappan, N.J.: Revell, 1984), 97.

4. Ibid., 99.

5. Robert Murray McCheyne, quoted in Packer, *Keep in Step with the Spirit*, 120.

CHAPTER 5

1. Gay, *The Way of the (Modern) World*, 2–5.

2. Ibid., 12.

3. James Davison Hunter, *Culture Wars* (New York: Basic Books, 1991). See also James Davison Hunter, *Before the Shooting Begins* (New York: The Free Press, 1994).

4. Samuel P. Huntington, *The Clash of Civilizations and the Remaking of World Order* (New York: W. W. Norton Publishers, 1996).

5. Charles Merrill Smith, *How to Become a Bishop without Being Religious* (Garden City, N.J.: Doubleday, 1965).

6. W. Andrew Hoffecker, ed., *Building a Christian World View*, vol. 1 (Phillipsburg, N.J.: Presbyterian and Reformed Publishing Company, 1986), ix.

7. William Law, *A Serious Call to a Devout and Holy Life*, ed. Paul G. Stanwood (New York: Paulist Press, 1978), 148.

8. George Barna, *The Second Coming of the Church* (Nashville: Word, 1998), 135.

9. Ibid., 135.

10. Charles Malik, *The Two Tasks* (Westchester, Ill.: Cornerstone Books, 1986), 32.

11. Paul Johnson, *To Hell with Picasso and Other Essays* (London: Phoenix, 1997), 183–84.

12. Jeffrey Selingo, "How Food and Memory Come Together," *The Chronicle of Higher Education* (30 July 1999): 7.

13. Leon Kass, *The Hungry Soul: Eating and the Perfecting of our Nature* (New York: The Free Press, 1999), quoted in Johnson, *To Hell with Picasso and Other Essays*, 183.

14. For further elaboration of this position, see chapter 7.

CHAPTER 6

1. Robert Coles, *Children of Crisis* (New York: Dell Publishing Company, 1967), 71.

2. Isaac Watts, *Psalms Carefully Suited to the Christian Worship* (New York: White, Gallagher and White, 1831), 37.

3. J. I. Packer, *Concise Theology* (Wheaton: Tyndale House, 1993), 34.

4. Quoted by William Messer, *The Theology of Calvin* (Philadelphia: Westminster Press, 1956), 70.

5. D. J. A. Caines, "The Image of God in Man," *Tyndale Bulletin* 19 (1968), 96.

6. *The Complete Poems of Percy Bysshe Shelley*, with notes by Mary Shelley (New York: The Modern Library, 1994), 589.

7. John Bartlett, ed., *Familiar Quotations* (Boston: Little, Brown, and Company, 1992), 443.

8. Sidney Lanier, *Poems of Sidney Lanier* (New York: Charles Scribner's Sons, 1904), 17.

CHAPTER 7

1. H. R. Rookmaker, *Modern Art and the Death of a Culture* (Downers Grove, Ill.: InterVarsity Press, 1971), 109.

2. Ibid., 150ff., 120.

3. Ibid., 194–95.

4. Quoted in James Houston, *I Believe in the Creator* (London: Hodder and Stoughton, 1979), 161.

5. Gene Edward Veith Jr., *State of the Arts: From Bezalel to Mapplethorpe* (Wheaton: Crossway Books, 1991), 90.

6. Ibid., 86.

7. Os Guiness, *Fit Bodies, Fat Minds: Why Evangelicals Don't Think and What to Do about It* (Grand Rapids: Baker, 1994), 62.

8. William D. Romanowski, *Pop Culture Wars: Religion and the Role of Entertainment in American Life* (Downers Grove, Ill.: InterVarsity Press, 1996).

9. Ibid., 48.

10. Rookmaker, *Modern Art and the Death of a Culture*, 228.

11. Anne Hollander, *Seeing through Clothes* (Berkeley: University of California Press, 1993), 452–53.

12. Stuart Ewen, *All Consuming Images: The Politics of Style in Contemporary Culture* (New York: Basic Books, 1988), 23.

13. George Truehart, "Welcome to the Next Church," *The Atlantic Monthly* (August 1996): 37.

14. Ibid., 44.

15. Pierre Babin, with Mercedes Iannone, trans. David Smith, *The New Era in Religious Communication* (Minneapolis: Fortress Press, 1991), 89–90, 122ff.

16. Gregory Wolf, *The New Religious Humanism* (New York: The Free Press, 1997), xi–xxv, 199–214.

17. C. S. Lewis, *They Asked for a Paper* (London: Geoffrey Bles, 1962), 206, 209.

Chapter 8

1. M. Scott Peck, *The Road Less Traveled* (New York: Simon and Schuster, 1978), 15.

2. J. R. R. Tolkien, *The Fellowship of the Ring* (Boston: Houghton Mifflin, 1982), 44.

SUGGESTED READING

Bayley, Lewis. *The Practice of Piety*. Morgan, Pa.: Soli Deo Gloria Publications, 1994.

Bridges, Jerry. *The Practice of Godliness*. Colorado Springs: NavPress, 1983.

Colson, Charles, and Nancy Pearcy. *How Now Shall We Live?* Wheaton: Tyndale House, 1999.

Ferguson, Sinclair. *Kingdom Life in a Fallen World: Living Out the Sermon on the Mount*. Colorado Springs: NavPress, 1986.

Foster, Richard. *Celebration of Discipline*. Rev. ed. New York: HarperSanFrancisco, 1988.

Foster, Richard J., and James Bryan Smith, eds. *Devotional Classics: Selected Readings for Individuals and Groups*. San Francisco: Harper Nelson, 1993.

Jeffrey, David Lyle, ed. *A Burning and a Shining Light: English Spirituality in the Age of Wesley*. Grand Rapids: Eerdmans, 1987.

———. *The Law of Love: English Spirituality in the Age of Wycliffe*. Grand Rapids: Eerdmans, 1988.

Law, William. *A Serious Call to a Devout and Holy Life*. Edited by Paul G. Stanwood. New York: Paulist Press, 1978.

Neff, LaVonne, et al., eds. *Practical Christianity*. New York: Guideposts, 1987.

Nouwen, Henri. *Life of the Beloved: Spiritual Living in a Secular World*. New York: Crossroad, 1992.

Packer, J. I. *Hot Tub Religion*. Wheaton: Tyndale House, 1987.

———. *Rediscovering Holiness*. Ann Arbor, Mich.: Vine Books, 1992.

Packer, J. I., and Wilkinson, Loren, eds. *Alive to God: Studies in Spirituality*. Downers Grove, Ill.: InterVarsity Press, 1992.

Peterson, Eugene. *A Long Obedience in the Same Direction: Discipleship in an Instant Society*. Downers Grove, Ill.: InterVarsity Press, 1980.

184

———. *Run with the Horses*. Downers Grove, Ill.: InterVarsity Press, 1983.

———. *Where Your Treasure Is: Psalms That Summon You from Self to Community*. Grand Rapids: Eerdmans, 1985.

Piper, John. *Desiring God: Meditations of a Christian Hedonist*. Portland, Ore.: Multnomah Press, 1986.

Ryle, John Charles. *Practical Religion*. London: James Clarke & Co., 1964.

Schaeffer, Francis. *True Spirituality*. Wheaton, Ill.: Tyndale House, 1971.

Taylor, Jeremy. *The Rule and Exercises of Holy Living and Dying*. London: George Routledge and Sons, 1894.

Wallace, Dewey D., Jr. *The Spirituality of the Later English Puritans*. Macon, Ga.: Mercer University Press, 1987.

White, John. *The Fight*. Downers Grove, Ill.: InterVarsity Press, 1980.

Whitney, Donald S. *Spiritual Disciplines for the Christian Life*. Colorado Springs: NavPress, 1991.

Willard, Dallas. *The Divine Conspiracy*. San Francisco: Harper & Row, 1998.

———. *The Spirit of the Disciplines*. San Francisco: Harper & Row, 1988.

Dr. Luder G. Whitlock Jr. graduated from the University of Florida, Westminster Theological Seminary, and Vanderbilt University. After serving pastorates in Florida and Tennessee, he joined the faculty of Reformed Theological Seminary in 1975. He became acting president in 1978 and president in 1979.

Dr. Whitlock was the executive director of the New Geneva Study Bible and has contributed to several other significant volumes including *The Evangelical Dictionary of Theology, The Practice of Confessional Subscription, Baker Encyclopedia of the Bible,* and *A Mighty Long Journey: On the Way to Racial Reconciliation.*